T

901

ONE SUMMER MORNING in 1588, an English sea captain raced up from Plymouth Harbour to a lawn where Sir Francis Drake and other senior naval officers were busy with a game of bowls. He had momentous news: "My lords, the Armada is sighted!" Quietly, Drake answered, "We have time to finish the game, and beat the Spaniards too."

The fleet that threatened Queen Elizabeth's England was the greatest ever to menace the security of the realm. With more than a hundred war ships, from galleons to barges, King Philip II planned to conquer England and restore the Catholic faith. And waiting on the Flemish coast was a giant army, poised for invasion once the Armada had cleared the English Channel.

This was the moment Drake had longed for, since his raid on Cadiz the year before. The English fleet was smaller, but by avoiding close engagements and relying on gunnery, it harried the Armada through the Channel, finally shattering the enemy formation with fire-ships off Calais. From that moment the battle was won, and the crippled Armada struggled slowly home to ignominy and disgrace.

Roger Hart reconstructs this heroic battle through a fascinating selection of eyewitness accounts, and pictures of the period, in an exciting addition to THE DOCUMENTARY HISTORY SERIES.

Frontispiece Plymouth at the time of the Spanish Armada.

Battle of the Spanish Armada

Roger Hart

"Their force is wonderful, great and strong, yet we pluck their feathers little by little . . ." **Lord Howard of Effingham on the Armada, 1588.**

WAYLAND PUBLISHERS · LONDON
G. P. PUTNAM'S SONS · NEW YORK

SBN: (England): 85340 239 6
SBN: (United States): 399-11147-6
Library of Congress Catalogue Card Number: 72-96883

Set in "Monophoto" Times and printed offset litho in Great Britain by
Page Bros (Norwich) Ltd, Norwich

Contents

The Illustrations

Dating

In 1588 two calendars were in use, the Old Style used by the English and the New Style used by the Spanish. There was a difference of ten numerals. The same day was therefore 19th July to the English and 29th July to the Spanish.

1 The Shadow of War

IN THE SPRING of 1588, the huge naval Armada of Philip II's Spain sailed out from its anchorage in the River Tagus. Under its commander, the Duke of Medina Sidonia, it was to attempt the invasion of England. Some men, seeing how the Armada had been crewed and trained, quietly whispered that it stood little chance of success against the English navy of Sir Francis Drake, John Hawkins and other brave and experienced sea captains. But alone in his great palace, the Escorial, in Madrid, surrounded by papers and secretaries, the King of Spain was confident of victory.

For not only was the Armada the greatest war fleet Spain had ever built, but Philip had a deep belief in his mission to conquer the Protestant – "heretic" – realm of England. Philip was the most powerful Catholic monarch in the world, and supported by the Pope in Rome he felt it his most solemn duty to re-establish the true Catholic faith wherever he could. *Philip's Crusade*

And there was also the matter of "piracy". He knew that Queen Elizabeth had for years turned a blind eye to the activities of English sailors – notably Sir Francis Drake – in plundering the treasure galleons of Spain as they brought back gold, silver and precious stones from South America. Philip felt that the time had come for once and all to strike a final crippling blow against his English enemies.

King Philip ruled, as well as Spain, a large part of the Netherlands. This would make an excellent base at which to assemble his invading army. Here, too, he made it clear beyond any doubt that only the Catholic religion was to be tolerated. *Spanish Netherlands*

11

Opposite Elizabeth I, Queen of England (1558–1603)

Writing to his representative at Antwerp, in the Spanish Netherlands, he said: "With regard to Holland and Zeeland or any other provinces or towns, the first step must be for them to receive and maintain *alone* the exercise of the Catholic religion, and to subject themselves to the Roman church, without tolerating the exercise of any other religion. And in this religion there is to be no flaw, no change, no liberty of conscience or religious peace, or anything of the sort. They are all to embrace the Catholic religion, and the exercise of that is alone to be permitted (1)."

Elizabeth excommuni- cated Many years before, in 1570, Pope Pius V had excommunicated Queen Elizabeth, with the idea of setting her subjects free from their oath of allegiance. Now it was rumoured that the Pope had taken away the title "defender of the faith" from Queen Elizabeth, and given it to King Philip of Spain, "giving him charge to invade England upon this condition, that he should enjoy the conquered realm, as a vassal and tributary to the see of Rome. To this purpose the said Pope proffered a million of gold, one half to be paid in ready money, and the half when the realm of England or any famous port thereof were subdued.

"And for the greater furtherance of the whole business, he dispatched one D. Allen an Englishman, whom he had made Cardinal for the same purpose, into the Low Countries. This Allen being enraged against his own native country, had the Pope's Bull translated into English, meaning upon the arrival of the Spanish fleet, to have it so published in England. By this Bull the excommunications of the two former Popes were confirmed, and the Queen's most sacred Majesty was most unjustly deprived of all princely titles and dignities, her subjects being called on to perform obedience to the Duke of Parma, and to the Pope's Legate (2)."

But this was little more than a legal formality. In fact, apart from some of the Catholics in England, most of the nation was firmly united under their great Queen. The historian Ubaldino wrote: "It is easier to find flocks of white crows than one Englishman who loves a foreigner."

Sir Francis Drake It was common knowledge that, in 1587, Philip had already done much to prepare his Armada for the invasion attempt. But Queen Elizabeth did not want war; she refused to believe that the

Sir Francis Drake, the most skilled of England's naval commanders

threat was a serious one. Sir Francis Drake thought otherwise. He had spent many years in naval skirmishes with Spanish ships, and was convinced of the danger of the Armada. He was a skilled captain, and brave commander, and was anxious to attack the Spanish before they tried to attack his own country.

We have a fascinating description of Drake, written by a Spanish nobleman: "He is called Francisco Drac, and is a man of

13

about 35 years of age, low of stature, with a fair beard, and is one of the greatest mariners that sail the seas, both as a navigator and as a commander. His vessel is a galleon of nearly 400 tons, and is a perfect sailor. She is manned with 100 men, all of service, and of an age for warfare, and all are as practised therein as old soldiers from Italy could be. Each one takes particular pains to keep his arquebus clean. He treats them with affection, and they treat him with respect.

"He carries with him nine or ten cavaliers, cadets of English noblemen. These form part of his council, which he calls together for even the most trivial matter, although he takes advice from no one. But he enjoys hearing what they say and afterwards issues his orders. He has no favourite... He is served on silver dishes with gold borders and gilded garlands, in which are his arms. He carries all possible dainties and perfumed waters. He said that many of these had been given to him by the Queen.

"None of these gentlemen took a seat or covered his head before him, until he repeatedly urged him to do so. This galleon of his carries about thirty heavy pieces of artillery and a great quantity of firearms with the requisite ammunition and lead. He dines and sups to music of viols. He carries trained carpenters and artisans, so as to be able to careen the ship at any time. Besides being new, the ship has a double lining. I understood that all the men he carries with him receive wages, because, when our ship was sacked, no man dared take anything without his orders. He shows them great favour, but punishes the least fault. He also carries painters who paint for him pictures of the coast in its exact colours... I managed to ascertain whether the General was well liked, and all said that they adored him (3)."

More news   Early in 1587, more and more reports poured in to Queen Elizabeth, about the preparations of the Armada. One spy reported: "The King of Spain has 100,000 men and victuals in readiness at Lisbon, and 7,000 Portuguese, all destined for the invasion of England." Other spies confirmed that there were now more than 100 ships awaiting orders to sail.

At last, Drake and other commanders persuaded Elizabeth that something must be done – and quickly. Drake was stationed at Plymouth with 25 ships, the largest fleet that Elizabeth had

14

The Catholic King Philip II of Spain saw the conquest of Protestant England as a sacred duty

Drake delayed the Armada by the destruction he caused to the Spanish
navy when he raided Cadiz in 1587

ever commissioned. The biggest vessel was Drake's flagship the
Elizabeth Bonaventure of 600 tons, and with a keel 100 feet
long. The fleet had about 2,200 seamen and soldiers ready to
go to sea.

Cadiz raid It was agreed that Drake should lead an expedition to attack
the Spanish Navy in its own ports. Down at Plymouth last minute
preparations were in progress. But back in London, Queen
Elizabeth was having a change of heart: some of her advisers
were saying that a raid now would only ruin the chances of peace
with Spain.

Drake feared that something like this might happen. With all
haste he took his fleet out to sea in the English Channel, at the
very moment that a royal messenger was riding post-haste
down to Plymouth with orders to cancel the expedition. Not even
the Queen could stop Drake now.

The appearance of the English fleet before Cadiz panicked the Spaniards

In April, Drake's fleet reached Cadiz, and in one of the most daring raids in naval history, sank and burned many Spanish ships as they lay helplessly at anchor. For years after, men spoke of the time when Drake had "singed the King of Spain's beard."

On 27th April Drake wrote to Walsingham, the Queen's Secretary, to report his victory: "The 19th we arrived into the road [anchorage] of Cadiz in Spain, where we found sundry great ships, some laden, some half-laden, and some ready to be laden with the King's provisions for England. We stayed there until the 21st, in which time we sank a Biscayan of 1,200 tons, burnt a ship of the Marquess of Santa Cruz of 1,500 tons, and 31 ships more of 1,000, 800, 600, 400 to 200 tons the piece. We carried away four with us laden with provisions, and departed thence at our pleasure, with as much honour as we could wish, even though during the time of our abode there we were both often fought by

17

twelve of the King's galleys, of whom we sank two, and always repulsed the rest. We were without ceasing vehemently shot at from the shore, but to our little hurt, God be thanked. Yet at our departure we were courteously written to by one Don Pedro, general of those galleys (4)."

When Drake had appeared at Cadiz, the town had been in uproar. The Duke of Medina Sidonia had ridden in from Jerez, to take over the defence of the town himself. He wished "the enemy would come out of their nests and prove if they were better at fighting than at creeping about in the dark attacking crewless ships which could not resist with more than their wooden hulls (5)."

Drake reports on Armada

It was obvious to Drake, after his raid, that the Armada was as big as everyone had feared. Writing to Walsingham he said: "I assure your honour such preparation was never heard of nor known as the King of Spain has and daily makes to invade England . . . which if they be not met before they join will be very perilous . . . This service, which by God's sufferance we have done, will breed some alterations . . . All possible preparations for defence are very expedient . . . I dare not almost write of the great forces we hear the King of Spain has. Prepare in England strongly, and most by sea! (6)"

But when Drake returned to London, he was to find that the faint-hearts were still advising Elizabeth to go on seeking a peace settlement. And if Drake had a hero's welcome from the people, he had a frosty reception at Court. Elizabeth was angry that he might have jeopardized the peace talks. Drake could hardly believe his ears. Was this any way to talk, when the greatest fleet Spain had ever put to sea was soon to darken the horizon?

2 Queen Elizabeth's Navy

THE SHIPS which Drake had seen in Cadiz were great towering galleons. Their size alone brought fear and terror into the hearts of their enemies. But Sir Walter Raleigh felt that England's smaller and faster ships had definite advantages: "We find by experience that the greatest ships are the least serviceable, go very deep to water, and of marvellous charge and cumber, our channels decaying every year. Besides, they are less nimble, less easy to handle, and very seldom employed . . . A ship of 600 tons will carry as good ordnance as a ship of 1,200 tons; and though the greater have double her number, the lesser will turn her broadsides twice before the greater can wind once. The high charging of ships brings them ill qualities, makes them extreme leeward, makes them sink deep in the water, makes them labour and makes them overset. Men of better sort and better breeding would be glad to find more steadiness and less tottering cage-work (7)." *Best size for ships*

Unlike her father, Henry VIII, Elizabeth had done little for the Navy. There was a chronic shortage of ships and supplies of all kinds. Also, since Elizabeth's treasury was nearly empty, it became necessary to levy forced loans on the richer citizens of England. These were unpopular, as one can imagine. No one could be sure when they would be repaid. This is an official letter from the government addressed to one Roger Columbell, asking him to lend £25: *Forced loans*

"Trusty and well-beloved, we greet you well. Whereas for the better withstanding of the intended invasion of this realm [by] the King of Spain . . . we are now forced for the defence of the

A tall Spanish war galleon, part of the Armada fleet

same, and of our good loving subjects, to be at infinite charges both by sea and land . . . We have therefore thought it expedient, having always our good and loving subjects most ready at such times to furnish us by way of loan some convenient portions of money, agreeable with their estate . . .

"We have also particularly named you, Roger Columbell, for your ability and goodwill you bear to us and our realm, to be one; wherefore we require you to pay to our use the sum of five-and-twenty pounds to such person as by our Lieutenant of that County shall be named to you by his handwriting (8)."

Lack of medical knowledge caused more problems for the Navy. Scurvy was an age-old disease suffered by sailors. It was caused by lack of vitamin C and fresh vegetables. Sir John Hawkins wrote that oranges and lemons seemed to have almost magical powers in curing disease at sea: "Coming aboard our ships, there was great joy amongst my company, and many with the sight of the oranges and lemons, seemed to recover heart. This is a wonderful secret of the power and wisdom of God, that has hidden so great and unknown virtue in this fruit, to be a certain remedy for this infirmity. I at once caused them all to be shared among our sick men, which were so many, that there were not more than three or four to a share (9)."

Scurvy

A physician called William Clowes thought there were many causes of scurvy. He wrote in his book on surgery: "This infection, as I gathered by enquiry, was reputed principally unto their rotten and unwholesome victuals. For they said their bread was musty and mouldy biscuit, their beer sharp and sour like vinegar, their water corrupt and stinking. The best drink they had, they called beveridge, half wine and half putrified water mingled together, and yet a very short and small allowance.

Causes of scurvy

"Their beef and pork was likewise, by reason of its corruption, a most loathsome and filthy taste and savour. Indeed they were forced to stop their noses when they did eat and drink thereof. Moreover their bacon was poor, their fish, butter and cheese wonderful bad, and so consequently all the rest of their victuals (10)."

One of the problems on a long voyage was to keep the seamen supplied with fresh water. Sir John Hawkins once solved this

Distilled water

problem by building a distillery on board ship: "Our fresh water had failed us many days, before we saw the shore, by reason of our long voyage, without touching any land, and the excessive drinking of the sick and diseased, which could not be done without. Yet with an invention I had in my ship, I easily drew out of the water of the sea sufficient quantity of fresh water to sustain my people, with little expense of fuel, for with four billets I stilled a hogshead of water, and therewith dressed the meat for the sick and healthy. The water so distilled we found to be wholesome and nourishing (11)."

Quack surgeons   William Clowes bitterly complained against the "travelling surgeons" who were no more than quacks. Often, they were the "principal surgeons for great ships of war, and in charge of numbers of men. They received aforehand, towards the preparation and furnishing of their surgery chests, some £20, and some £40 and £50. But, in conclusion, they falsified their promises, for shortly after they had received their money, they . . . ran away, and could not be found nor heard of, until the captains that hired them had set sail and gone forward on their great and long voyages, without any surgeon at all (12)."

Gunnery   The power of the English Navy depended upon her gunners. The following is from a gunnery handbook of the time: "A gunner ought to be a sober, wakeful, lusty, hardy, patient, prudent, and quick-spirited man. He ought also to have a good eyesight, a good judgment, and perfect knowledge to select a convenient place in the day of service, to plant his ordnance where he may do most hurt unto the enemies, and be least annoyed by them.

"Also, a gunner in time of service ought to forbid with meek and courteous speeches all manner of persons, other than his appointed assistants, to come near his pieces, so that none of his pieces may be choked, poisoned, or hurt. And he ought not for any prayers or reward to lend any piece of his gunmatch to another person, because it may be very hurtful to him in time of service to lack the same. . .

"Every gunner who shall serve upon the sea in any ship ought [to tell] the owner or captain of the vessel in which he shall serve, the weight and price of so much gunpowder, and of so

The clothes worn by an English
sailor at the time of the Armada

The increased range of English naval artillery played a decisive part in the
Armada's defeat

many fit pellets, as will be enough to charge all the pieces in his
vessel forty times over, and also the price of ten barrels or more
of gunpowder, which he ought to have for the only making of
fireworks (13)."

The handbook set out the subjects which a gunner should be
familiar with:

"How the makers of gunpowder do mingle together the things
of which they make gunpowder.

"How great pieces of artillery are named; and how, through
the intolerable fault of careless or unskilled gun-founders, all
our great pieces of one name are not of one length, nor of one
weight, nor of one height in their mouths.

"How you may cause any great piece of artillery to make in
his discharge an exceeding great noise and a marvellous roar.

"How you may know what number of feet, yards, paces, or
scores, any piece of artillery will shoot in an unsensible crooked
line, or (as the gunner's term is) at point blank.

"How you may make hollow balls of metal, which, being shot
out of great ordnance or mortar pieces, or thrown with slings
out of men's hands among soldiers standing or marching in

Fire arrows shot from small artillery played havoc among the wooden
warships of the Tudor period

battle, will suddenly break in many pieces and do great harm . . .

"How you may make divers sorts of fireworks, which, being
shot in a dark night out of a mortar piece, or out of any other
piece of artillery, or thrown out of men's hands will give so great
a light that you may discern whether or no any enemies are in
or near that place.

"To make rockets or squibs, which, being thrown up into the
air, will cast forth flames of fire, and in coming down towards
the ground will show like stars falling from heaven . . .

"To know, by the help of a Gunner's Semicircle, how many
miles, paces, yards, or feet any ship lying at road in the sea, or
tower, or any other mark upon the land in sight, is from you (14)."

Ships that were at sea for months at a time sometimes had their *Damage to*
hulls eaten away by a kind of sea worm. As one writer noted, *hulls*
these "in all hot countries, enter into the planks of ships, and
especially where are rivers of fresh water; for the common
opinion is that they are bred in fresh water, and with the current
of the rivers are brought into the sea. But experience teaches that
they breed in the great seas in all hot climates, especially near the
equinoctial line. For lying so long under and near the line, and

25

towing a shalop at our stern, coming to cleanse her in Brazil, we found her all under water covered with these worms, as big as the little finger of a man, on the outside of the plank, not fully covered, but half the thickness of their body, like a jelly, wrought into the plank as with a gouge (15)."

State of the Navy   The Admiralty was concerned about naval security. The Tudor age was famous for the spirit of its merchant adventurers, who sailed to all parts of the world. But these "private voyages

Gonne powder·   Shotte of yron   Shotte of stoen   Bolbes· Bol
                                      and· leade·   knowes· Mozt
                                                         By slyby· one

A four-masted English man-o'-war with two gun decks

have proved prejudicial to her Majesty's designs. For often they that go in such ships are taken prisoners and give light and knowledge of our designs (16)."

The same report added: "There are so many abuses in her Majesty's ships that the reforming of one is to little purpose, unless there be a reformation in the whole. And I will first begin with victuals, in which consist the lives of men. In this there is such great abuse in every voyage that there is no man but has

A smaller English warship with only one gun deck

cause to complain. The gunners, into whose charge is commited the strength of the ship, are preferred to their places rather for money than merit.

"And to descend to the ships themselves, there are so many impediments in them in our southern voyages that we cannot say anything is strong or serviceable about them. And though their wants be made known before their going from home, the officers of the Navy . . . have not that care which they should. And lastly, the men that serve in them are so evilly treated that they say it is the only thing that makes them backward to serve the Queen (17)."

Remedies   But what were the remedies for all this? It was "to execute severe justice upon the chief men in office. First the Victualler, if he fail either in goodness or quantity of her Majesty's allowance; let his life answer it, for no subject's estate is able to make up the damage her Majesty may sustain by such defect. And to take away all excuses of his part, and to provide there may be no failing of the service, it would be convenient to have a surplus of victuals transported in other ships, to be exchanged, if upon view the other prove to be ill-conditioned.

"Secondly, for the gunners: their shortage of powder and shot, and other things under their charge, are intolerable; and they have been the more emboldened by the baseness of some captains who have consented to their theft.

"To reform this, it would be good to have a deputy appointed in every ship from the Officers of the Ordnance, to take charge of powder, shot, and all other things, and to deliver them to such men as shall be accountable for them at the end of the voyage. For it is unreasonable that so great a charge should be committed to the gunners, who make no conscience to steal, and may steal without control when it is in their possession.

"Another thing a captain must have orders to forbid, and look precisely for it be obeyed, is the lavish use of shooting for pleasure at the meeting of ships, passing by castles, and banqueting aboard. For indeed there is more powder wastefully spent in this sort than against an enemy.

"For the third, which is the disability of ships to the south-ward, it is caused by the great weight of ordnance, which

The Seamans Srecets.

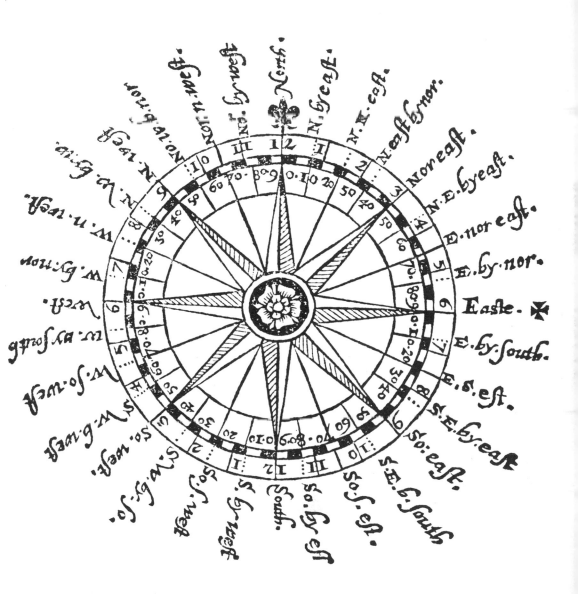

A Tudor rose decorates this English sailor's compass

makes them laboursome and causes their weakness. And, seeing how few gunners are allowed to every ship, it would be better to leave some of these pieces at home rather than pester the ships with them.

"Indeed all her Majesty's ships are far undermanned. For when people come to be divided into three parts, one third to tackle the ship, the other to ply their small shot, and the third to use their ordnance, all the three services fail for want of men to execute them.

"Neither do I see that more men can be contained in the Queen's ships . . . for want of stowage for victuals and room to lodge in. No ship that returns from the south should go to sea again under half a year's respite in harbour. In this time she will be well aired, and her ballast must be changed . . .

"And lastly, for the men—for without them ships are not available—their treatment has been so ill that it is no marvel they show unwillingness to serve the Queen. For if they return sick from any voyage such is the charity of the people ashore that they will sooner die than find pity, unless they bring money with them.

"And seeing her Majesty must, and does, pay all men that serve her, it were better for them, and much more profit and honour to the Queen, to discharge them on their first landing, than to keep them longer unpaid. For whether they are sick, or lie idle in harbour, their entertainment runs on till they be discharged, to the great consumption of victuals and wages, which falls upon the Queen (18)."

But the problems remained. The task of reforming the Navy, in the face of scores of conflicting vested interests, proved too great. And Elizabeth's Navy put to sea against the great Spanish Armada with all her senior officers, like Drake, complaining bitterly about the shortage of supplies and other abuses.

3 Beacons on the Coasts

ENGLAND was no easy country to invade. A famous English writer, Thomas Platter, said "it is extremely difficult to land in England, since there are only five ports in the whole realm, all very well and securely fortified to prevent any enemy from approaching. Thus, as soon as anything is sighted at sea—for battleships are always anchored at the ports keeping watch there —a signal is given at the ports with a burning pan of resin. This is straightaway observed inland, for the country is flat for the most part; and throughout the entire kingdom pans of resin are set up on little mounds, and watch kept there day and night. As soon as a signal is given it travels over the whole country, so that roughly speaking, in a trice the report goes round of what is happening at sea (19)."

There were two ways of defending the island of Britain. One was to ignore command of the sea, and concentrate on defending the coasts with an army. The other was to build up the Navy, so that no invading force could ever set foot on British soil. Raleigh did not agree with Platter. He was emphatic that control of the sea was more vital: *Army versus Navy*

"It is impossible for any maritime country, not having the coasts admirably fortified, to defend itself against a powerful enemy that is master of the sea. I say that such an army cannot be resisted on the coast of England, without a fleet to impeach it [face it]."

Even suppose "that Kent is able to furnish 12,000 foot, and that those 12,000 be laid in the three best landing places within that country, to wit, 3,000 at Margate, 3,000 at the Ness, and

English coastal defences. The burning lanterns signalled that the Armada
had been sighted

6,000 at Folkestone, that is somewhat equally distant from them both. And suppose that two of these troops be directed to strengthen the third, when they shall see the enemy's fleet to bend towards it." Even so, "if the enemy, setting sail from the Isle of Wight in the first watch of the night, and towing their longboats at their sterns, shall arrive by dawn of day at the Ness, and thrust their army on shore there; it will be hard for those 3,000 that are at Margate (24 long miles from thence) to come soon enough to reinforce their fellows at the Ness.

"Nay, how shall they at Folkestone be able to do it, who are nearer by more than half the way?—seeing that the enemy, at his first arrival, will either make his entrance by force, with three or four hundred shot of great Artillery, and quickly put the first 3,000, that were entrenched at the Ness, to run; or else give them so much to do that they shall be glad to send for help to Folkestone, and perhaps to Margate, whereby those places will be left bare.

"Now let us suppose that all the 12,000 Kentish soldiers arrive at the Ness before the enemy can be ready to disembark his army, so that he shall find it unsafe to land in the face of so many. Yet must we believe that he will play the best of his own game, and under cover of night set sail towards the East: what shall hinder him to take ground, either at Margate, the Downs, or elsewhere, before they at the Ness can be well aware of his departure? Certainly, there is nothing more easy than to do it.

"The like may be said of Weymouth, Purbeck, Poole, and of all landing places on the south coast. For every man knows that ships, without putting themselves out of breath, will easily outrun the soldiers that coast them . . . A fleet of ships may be seen at sunset, and after it, at the Lizard; yet by the next morning they may recover Portland. But an army of foot shall not be able to march it in six days (20)."

A Council of War was held in London in 1587, to discuss the security of the realm. If a great fleet was to sail from Spain, to attempt an invasion, where would it try to land on English soil? The Council looked at the possibilities one by one, and considered how best to defend them:

Council of War: 1587

"For Plymouth, both by fortification and assembly of people.

A view of London at the time of the Spanish Armada

ON

Merchantaylors

Haberdashers

Salters.

Ironmongers

Vintners.

Clothworkers

Scala paſſuum 5 pedum

80   160   240   320   400   480

Spitle fylder

Fluuius

Bellyns gate
Galley kaye
Iron kaye
Custom house
The tower
S. Katherynes

Earl Southlu

S. Towleyes

Olde Swanne
Winchester houſe

Sermaſhſerge houſe
Maryeouerryes

Southwarke

35

36

In Devon and Cornwall there are of trained men in the counties 6,000 men, which are to be assembled for the defence of Plymouth, standing equally to both counties . . . Two thousand of those should be assembled together at Plymouth, under such a General as shall be ordained to govern that western army, to the intent that they may know their leaders, be acquainted with watch and ward, and be thoroughly instructed to all purposes, that on alarm there may be no amaze, nor any confusion . . .

Plymouth

"For Portland, by assembling of men and fortifying. In Dorset and Wiltshire there are of trained men 2,700 which are to be assembled for the defence of that place, and that 2,000 of the said number should be assembled and exercised, as before is said, at Plymouth, or in some place of Wiltshire appointed. For the Isle of Wight to take Somersetshire, in which there are 2,000 footmen.

Portland

"At Sandwich, and the Downs, by the assembling of men. In Kent and Sussex there are of trained men 4,500, which are to be assembled in those places for defence thereof; and 2,000 of the said number to be assembled at Sandwich, to be governed and exercised, as before is said, for Plymouth.

Sandwich

"So likewise for Norfolk and Suffolk like order to be observed . . .

"These garrisons shall remain but for twenty days, to be thoroughly trained and acquainted with encamping. And then every such 2,000 men in garrison, being so acquainted with this discipline, shall give example to a great army of raw men, whereby there shall be no manner of confusion on all alarms.

"Further, we are of opinion that to these 2,000 there shall be twenty captains appointed, which twenty captains having each of them 100 trained men, shall receive under their charge, when the army shall assemble, 100 more. So as in effect there shall be 4,000 men in order, and under martial discipline. The choice of these captains we think, for the one half, should be left to the choice of the General of the army, and the other ten to be of the principal gentlemen of the country, under whom there may be soldiers appointed for their lieutenants (21)."

The Council was especially worried about the safety of the Queen. "Because there is a special regard to be had to the safe-

Queen's safety

Opposite A Tudor gunner: if the Spanish landed, the defence of the realm would depend on the small English army

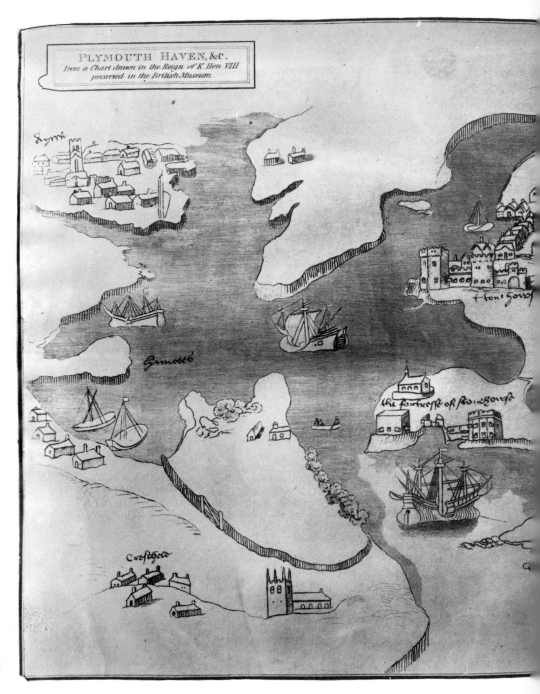

A map of Plymouth Haven

Plymouth

Chowgete hill

The foutnesse of plymouth

Catte wather

39

guard of her Majesty's person, we think it most necessary that an army should be provided to that end, to be made up of such counties as are appointed and reserved for that purpose, and to join with the forces of the City of London, and such other as may be armed out of her Majesty's store (22)."

The Council then considered the defence of the three places where the Spanish seemed most likely to head for:

"Milford . . . There should be a trained number of 2,000 footmen and 500 horse, to be levied and had in readiness. And for the increase of horsemen, if any lack be, then the gentlemen with their serving men may be commanded to supply the default to the number aforesaid.

"Plymouth. The reason why Plymouth is thought to be the most likely place, is that it is unlikely that the King of Spain will engage his fleet too far within the Sleeve before he has mastered one good harbour. Of these Plymouth is the nearest to Spain, easily to be won, speedily to be by him fortified, and conveniently situated to send help to, either out of Spain or France.

"Portland. The reason why Portland is also an apt place to land in, is that there is a great harbour for all his ships to ride in, and good landing for men. The isle being won is a strong place for retreat, the country adjoining open fields, where with great ease he may march with his whole army.

"The reason why the Downs, Margate, and the River Thames are thought fit landing places, is in respect of the ease of landing, and nearness to the Prince of Parma, in whose forces the King of Spain reposes special trust (23)."

On 21st December, 1587, Queen Elizabeth commissioned Lord Howard as Lord High Admiral, in readiness for the worst that might happen. He was given power to "lead and command all . . . our said fleet or army . . . in this present service for resisting and destroying the Spaniards and others . . . attempting . . . any design against our kingdoms [and] to invade, enter, spoil and make himself master of the kingdoms . . . belonging to the said Spaniards and others [and] with force of arms to spoil, offend, repress, subdue . . . the Spaniards (24)."

Until the time of the Armada crisis, Drake had been the Admiral of the West, and flown an Admiral's flag. But when the

Charles Howard, Lord High Admiral of England

English fleet was placed under Lord Howard, Howard was appointed Admiral, and Drake his Vice-Admiral. When Howard brought his ships down to Plymouth to meet Drake, he brought a Vice Admiral's flag for him.

Drake accepted his position calmly. He hoisted the new flag "with military ceremonial, showing a suitable deference as befitted their respective ranks. And he showed himself always of one mind and thought with the senior Admiral". The government was relieved, "because it might have been supposed that, being reduced in rank and in the substance of his authority by such a ceremony, Sir Francis Drake, a man born and grown up among freebooters, would have found it irksome to practise the self-restraint admired by the ancient Romans (25)."

While the Privy Council attended to the defence of the south coast, Drake and other sea captains were forced to kick their heels in Plymouth. Putting garrisons in the ports was all very well. But, as Raleigh had pointed out, no one knew where the Armada might try to land. And soldiers could not be moved fast enough along the south coast, to keep up with an enemy fleet at sea.

Surely, said Drake, precious time was being wasted. Why hold out for a peace which would never come? Let Queen Elizabeth only give the word, and the Armada could be attacked in the open sea, or in its harbours, and shattered before it came within twenty leagues of English soil.

4 *Arguments and Delays*

1ST JANUARY, 1588. The New Year came, and still the English fleet was anchored at Plymouth. In February, the debate was still going on: were the Spanish serious in their continuing proposals for peace? Or was it all a blind, a smokescreen behind which they were preparing for the greatest onslaught ever known by one naval power against another?

On 1st February, Sir John Hawkins wrote to Walsingham, the Queen's Secretary, from aboard the *Bonaventure*. He agreed that people wanted peace, if possible: "But in my poor judgment the right way is not taken. . . . We have to choose either a dishonourable and uncertain peace, or to put on virtuous and valiant minds, to make a way through with such a settled war as may bring forth and command a quiet peace. This peace which we have in hand has little likelihood to be good for us, but to win a better time for them (26)."

On 21st February, Lord Howard told Lord Burghley that the fleet was in a good seaworthy condition. "I have been aboard of every ship that goes out with me, and in every place where any may creep, and I do thank God that they be in the state they be in. There is none of them that knows what a leak means. I have known when an Admiral of England has gone out, and two ships in the fleet could not say so. There is none that goes out now that I would not dare go to the Rio de la Plate in her (27)."

Seaworthy fleet

Eight days later he wrote again: "I think there were never in any place in the world worthier ships than these are, for so many. And as few as we are, if the King of Spain's forces be not hundreds, we will make good sport with them (28)."

43

Queen Elizabeth with her chief minister, Lord Burghley and secretary
Sir Francis Walsingham

At the same time Admiral Sir William Winter was writing: "Our ships do show themselves like gallants here. I assure you it will do a man's heart good to behold them. Would to God the [enemy] were upon the seas with all his forces, and we in the view of them; then I doubt not but that you should hear that we would make his enterprise very unpleasant to him (29)."

On 30th March, Sir Francis Drake wrote to the Privy Council, *Drake's* urging them to take the initiative, and seek the Spanish out: *impatience* "If her Majesty and your Lordships think that the King of Spain means any invasion in England, then doubtless his force is and will be great in Spain. There he will make his groundwork or foundation, whereby the Prince of Parma may have the better entrance, which in my judgment is most to be feared. But if there may be any stop made of this fleet in Spain, that they may not come through the seas as conquerors – which, I assure myself, they think to do – then shall the Prince of Parma be checked (30)."

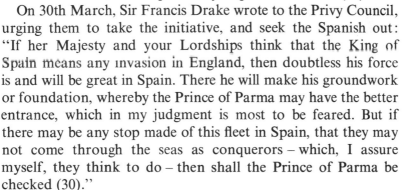

Parma was in command of a huge army being formed in the Spanish Netherlands. It was this army which would attempt the invasion, once the Armada had won control of the English Channel.

Drake urged the Council to strengthen the fleet at Plymouth as much as they possibly could. He gave two reasons: "First, because they are like to strike the first blow. And secondly, it will put great and good hearts into her Majesty's loving subjects, both abroad and at home. For they will be persuaded . . . that the Lord of all strength will put into her Majesty and her people courage and boldness not to fear any invasion in her own country, but to seek God's enemies and her Majesty's where they may be found . . .

"I must crave pardon of your good Lordships again and again, for my conscience has caused me to put my pen to the paper. And as God in his goodness has put my hand to the plough, so in His mercy it will never suffer me to turn back from the truth (31)."

He added, "The advantage and gain of time and place will be the only and chief means for our good . . . I most humbly beseech your good Lordships to persevere as you have begun, for with fifty sail of shipping we shall do more good upon their own coast, than a great many more will do here at home. And the sooner we are gone, the better we shall be able to impeach [try] them (32)."

Drake ended his letter with one of his many pleas for urgently needed ammunition: "I have sent to your good Lordships the note of such powder and munition as are delivered to us for this great service. This, in truth, I judge to be just a third part of that which is needful. For if we should lack it when we have most need of it, it will be too late to send to the Tower for it. I assure your Honours it neither is, or shall be, spent in vain (33)."

Throughout March, Queen Elizabeth and her Council hesitated. Lord Admiral Howard was still on the River Thames, and Drake still awaited his orders down at Plymouth. The more time passed, the stronger the Armada would become. On 13th April, 1588, Drake wrote a famous letter to Queen Elizabeth, begging her to give the word for action:

"I assure your Majesty, I have not in my lifetime known better men, and possessed with gallanter minds, than your Majesty's people are for the most part, which are here gathered together, voluntarily to put their hands and hearts to the finishing of this great piece of work . . . We are all persuaded that God, the giver of all victories, will in mercy look upon your most excellent Majesty, and us your poor subjects, who for the defence of your Majesty, our religion, and native country, have resolutely vowed the hazard of our lives.

"The advantage of time and place in all martial actions is half the victory, which if lost is irrecoverable. Wherefore, if your Majesty will command me away with those ships which are here already, and the rest to follow with all possible expedition, I hold it in my poor opinion the surest and best course."

And he begged the Queen to command "that they bring with them victuals sufficient for themselves and us, to the intent the service be not utterly lost for want thereof . . . For an Englishman, being far from his country, and seeing a present want of victuals to ensue, and perceiving no benefit to be looked for, but only blows, will hardly be brought to stay . . .

46

Opposite An English musketeer. Perennially short of money, England's land forces would have been hard put to hold off a Spanish invasion

"Touching my poor opinion how strong your Majesty's fleet should be to encounter this great force of the enemy, may God increase your most excellent Majesty's forces both by sea and land daily. For this I surely think: there was never any force so strong as there is now ready, or making ready, against your Majesty and true religion (34)."

Firing a cannon. While the Anglo-Spanish peace talks went on Spain built up her forces, but Elizabeth and her advisers kept the English commanders short of men, material and money

5 The Great Armada

WHILE QUEEN ELIZABETH and her Privy Council were delaying in London, the Spanish were wasting no time. For several years, the Armada had been in active preparation. Its commander was Alvarez de Bassano, the Marquis of Santa Cruz. Santa Cruz was one of Spain's great naval heroes. He had been the victor over the Turks at the famous Battle of Lepanto in 1571, and had recently won an important victory over the Portuguese in the Azores.

The Marquis was full of enthusiasm for the invasion of England. His target was to build up a fleet, of more than 500 ships, and a force of seamen and soldiers of about 94,000. His plan was to build up a large invasion force in the Spanish Netherlands, under the Duke of Parma, which would invade England at the mouth of the River Thames once the "invincible armada" had won control of the English Channel.

Richard Hakluyt wrote at the time: "A very large and particular description of this Navy was put in print and published by the Spaniards, in which were set down the number, names, and burdens of the ships, the number of mariners and soldiers throughout the whole fleet. Likewise the quantity of their ordnance, of their armour, of bullets, of match, of gun-powder, of victuals, and of all their naval furniture was [given].

Hakluyt on the Armada

"Unto all these were added the names of the governors, captains, noblemen and gentlemen volunteers, of whom there was so great a multitude, that scarce was there any family of account, or any one principal man throughout all Spain, that had not a brother, son or kinsman in that fleet. All of them were

49

Overleaf A towering Spanish galleon of the time of the Armada

in good hope to purchase to themselves in that navie (as they termed it) invincible, endless glory and renown, and to possess themselves of great lordships and riches in England, and in the Low Countries. But because the said description was translated and published out of Spanish into divers other languages, we will here only make [a summary] thereof.

"Portugal furnished and set forth . . . ten galleons, two zabraes, 1,300 mariners, 3,300 soldiers, 300 great pieces, with all requisite furniture.

"Biscay, under the conduct of John Martines de Ricalde, Admiral of the whole fleet, set forth ten galleons, 4 pataches, 700 mariners, 2,000 soldiers, 250 great pieces, &c.

"Guipusco, under the conduct of Michael de Oquendo, ten galleons, 4 pataches, 700 mariners, 2,000 soldiers, 310 great pieces.

"Italy with the Levant Islands, under Martine de Vertendona, 10 galleons, 800 mariners, 2,000 soldiers, 310 great pieces, &c.

"Castile, under Diego Flores de Valdez, 14 galleons, two pataches, 1,700 mariners, 2,400 soldiers, and 380 great pieces, &c.

"Andalusia, under the conduct of Petro de Valdez, 10 galleons, one patache, 800 mariners, 2,400 soldiers, 280 great pieces, &c.

"Item, under the conduct of John Lopez de Medina, 23 great Flemish hulks, with 700 mariners, 3,200 soldiers, and 400 great pieces.

"Item, under Hugo de Moncada, four galleasses containing 1,200 galley-slaves, 460 mariners, 870 soldiers, 200 great pieces, &c.

"Item, under Diego de Mandrana, four galleys of Portugal, with 888 galley-slaves, 360 mariners, 20 great pieces, and other requisite furniture.

"Item, under Antonio de Mendoza, 22 pataches and zabraes, with 574 mariners, 488 soldiers, and 193 great pieces (35)."

Size of ships   This was not all: "Besides these ships there were 20 caravels rowed with oars, being appointed to perform necessary services to the greater ships: so that all the ships of this Navy amounted to the sum of 150, each one being sufficiently provided of

52

furniture and victuals.

"The number of mariners in the said fleet were above 8,000; of slaves, 2,088; of soldiers, 20,000, besides noblemen and gentlemen volunteers. The ships were of a huge and incredible capacity. For the whole fleet was large enough to contain the burden of 60,000 tons.

"The galleons were 64 in number, being of a huge size, and very stately built, being of marvellous force also, and so high, that they resembled great castles, most fit to defend themselves and to withstand any assault. But in giving any other ships the encounter they were far inferior to the English and Dutch ships, which can with great dexterity wield and turn themselves at all attempts. The upperwork of the said galleons was of thickness and strength sufficient to bear off musket shot. The lower work and timbers were out of measure strong, being framed of planks and ribs four or five foot thick, so that no bullets could pierce them, but such as were discharged hard at hand. This afterward proved true, for a great number of bullets were found to stick fast within those thick planks. Great and well pitched cables were twined about the masts of their ships, to strengthen them against the battery of shot.

"The galleasses were so big that they contained within them chambers, chapels, turrets, pulpits . . . The galleasses were rowed with great oars, there being in each one of them 300 slaves for the same purpose, and were able to do great service with the force of their ordnance. All these . . . were furnished and beautified with trumpets, streamers, banners, warlike ensigns, and other such ornaments (36)."

Hakluyt also described how the Armada was armed: *Arms*

"Their pieces of brass ordnance were 1,600 and of iron 1,000. The bullets thereto belonging were 120,000. Item of gunpowder 5,600 quintals. Of match 1,200 quintals. Of muskets and calivers 7,000. Of halberts and partisans 10,000. Moreover, they had great store of cannons, double-cannons, culverins and field-pieces for land services (37)."

The English fleet put its faith in the speed of its ships and the *Spanish* heavy firepower of its guns. But the Spaniards regarded naval *tactics* battles as land battles at sea. They took thousands of soldiers

53

Overleaf The vast Armada sailing in formation up the English Channel

with them, intending to come alongside the ships of the English fleet, and win the battle by boarding them and taking the crews prisoner.

As Hakluyt wrote, "The Spaniards, in their armadas by sea, imitate the discipline, order, and officers, which are in an army by land, and divide themselves into three bodies: to wit, soldiers, mariners, and gunners.

"Their soldiers ward and watch, and their officers in every ship round, as if they were on the shore. This is the only task they undergo, except cleaning their arms . . . The gunners are exempted from all labour and care, except about the artillery. And these are either Germans, Flemings, or strangers, for the Spaniards are poorly practised in this art. The mariners are but as slaves to the rest, to moil and to toil day and night. And these are few and bad, and not suffered to sleep or harbour themselves under the decks. For in fair or foul weather, in storms, sun, or rain, they must go without shelter or succour.

"The gunners fight only with their great artillery. The mariners attend only to the tackling of the ship and handling of the sails, and are unarmed, and subject to all misfortunes. They are not permitted to shelter themselves, but must stay aloft, whether it be necessary or not. So ordinarily, those which first fail are the mariners and sailors, of which they have the greatest need (38)."

Marines The Armada contained five *terzaes* (regiments) of soldiers as well as the seamen. They were "under the command of five governors termed by the Spaniards Masters of the Field, and amongst the rest there were many old and expert soldiers chosen out of the garrisons of Sicily, Naples, and Terçera. Their captains or colonels were Diego Pimentelli, Don Francisco de Toledo, Don Alonço de Luçon, Don Nicolas de Isla, Don Augustin de Mexico, who each had 32 companies under their conduct. Besides which there were many bands also of Castilians and Portuguese, every one of which had their own governors, captains, officers, colours and weapons.

"It was not lawful for any man, under heavy penalty, to carry any women or harlots in the fleet, and so the women hired certain ships, in which they sailed after the Navy: some

56

of which, driven by tempest, arrived upon the coast of France (39)."

But the Spanish were to find – to their cost – that the choice of tactics would rest with the faster English ships, who could take full advantage of their heavier fire power. King Philip was aware of the strength of English gunnery, and warned his commanders about it:

"The enemy's object will be to fight at long distance, because of his advantage in artillery, and the many artificial fires with which he will be furnished. The aim of our men, on the contrary, must be to bring him to close quarters and grapple with him, and you will have to be very careful to have this carried out. For your information a statement is sent to you describing how the enemy employs his artillery, in order to deliver his fire low and sink his opponent's ships. And you will take such precautions as you consider necessary in this respect (40)."

The Armada was, of course, an invasion fleet. The arrangements for transport were very detailed, as Hakluyt tells us: *Invasion details* "They were provided with everything needed on land to carry their furniture from place to place, such as carts, wheels, wagons, &c. Also they had spades, mattocks and baskets to set pioneers to work. They had in like sort great store of mules and horses, and whatever else was requisite for a land army. They were so well stored of biscuit, that for the space of half a year, they might allow each person in the whole fleet half a quintal every month. The whole sum amounted to 100,000 quintals.

"Likewise of wine they had 147,000 pipes, sufficient also for half a year's expedition. Of bacon 6,500 quintals. Of cheese 3,000 quintals. Besides fish, rice, beans, pease, oil, vinegar, etc.

"Moreover they had 12,000 pipes of fresh water, and all other necessary provision, such as candles, lanterns, lamps, sails, hemp, ox-hides and lead to stop holes that might be made with the battery of gunshot. To be short, they brought all things expedient either for a fleet by sea, or for an army by land.

"This navy was esteemed by the King himself to contain 32,000 persons, and to cost him every day 30,000 ducats (41)."

Among the officers in the fleet were some young gentlemen who were going for the experience and adventure: "Over and besides the forenamed governors and officers . . . there were 124 very noble and worthy gentlemen, who went voluntarily at their own costs and charges, to the end they might see fashions, learn experience, and attain glory. Among them was the Prince of Ascoli, Alonzo de Leiva, the Marquis de Pennafiel, the Marquis de Ganes, the Marquis de Barlango, Count de Paredes, Count de Yelvas, and divers other marquises and earls of the honourable families of Mendoza, Toledo, Pachieco, Cordova, Guzman, Manricques, and a great number of others (42)."

The Armada also contained medical and spiritual helpers: "Martin Alorcon was appointed Vicar General of the Inquisition, being accompanied with more than a hundred monks, to wit, Jesuits, Capuchines, and mendicant friars. Besides whom there were also physicians, surgeons, apothecaries, and whatever else pertained to the hospital (43)."

Many neutral observers thought that, despite its size and all the preparations, the Armada would not be a match for the English. An Italian ambassador wrote that Philip II "very well knows how much consideration ought to be paid to such a fleet as the English fleet, both on account of its size, and also because the English are men of another mettle from the Spaniards, and enjoy the reputation of being . . . expert and active in all naval operations, and great sea dogs (44)."

The Pope thought much the same: "The King goes trifling with this Armada of his, but the Queen [Elizabeth] acts in earnest. Were she only a Catholic she would be our best beloved, for she is of great worth. Just look at Drake! Who is he? What forces has he? And yet he burned twenty-five of the King's ships at Gibraltar, and as many again at Lisbon; he has robbed the flotilla and sacked San Domingo. His reputation is so great that his countrymen flock to him to share his booty. We are sorry to say it, but we have a poor opinion of this Spanish Armada, and fear some disaster . . .

"The Queen of England has no need of the Turk to help her. Have you heard how Drake with his fleet has offered battle to the Armada? with what courage! do you think he showed any fear? He is a great captain (45)."

6 The Army of the Netherlands

THE PREPARATIONS for the Armada were not confined to the Iberian peninsula. The Low Countries – which formed part of Philip's dominions – were used, too: partly for men and supplies, partly to provide bases.

"While the Spaniards were furnishing their navy, the Duke of Parma, at the direction of King Philip, made great preparation in the Low Countries, to give aid and assistance to the Spaniards; building ships for the same purpose, and sending for pilots and shipwrights out of Italy.

"In Flanders he caused certain deep channels to be made, *Harbour works* and among the rest the channel of Yper commonly called Yper-lee, employing some thousands of workmen about that service, so that by this channel he might transport ships from Antwerp and Ghent to Bruges, where he had assembled above a hundred small ships called hoyes, being well stored with victuals. These hoyes he was determined to have brought into the sea by the way of Sluys, or else to have conveyed them by the said Yper-lee, being now of greater depth, into any port of Flanders.

"In the River Waten he caused 70 ships with flat bottoms to *Ships and men* be built, each to carry 30 horses. Each of them had bridges likewise for the horses to come on board, or to go forth on land. Of the same fashion he had provided 200 other vessels at Neiuport, but not so great. And at Dunkirk he procured 28 ships of war, such as were there to be had, and caused a sufficient number of mariners to be levied at Hamburg, Bremen, Emden, and at other places. He put in the ballast of the said ships, great

59

store of beams of thick planks, being hollow and set with iron pikes beneath. But on each side full of clasps and hooks, to join them together (46)."

The Duke of Parma knew that, if the Armada managed to reach the English coast, a great army would have to be landed. They would have to be able to defend their bridgeheads, and seize English ports. And so, "He had likewise at Gravelines provided 20,000 casks, which in a short space might be made joined together with nails and cords, and made into a bridge. To be short, whatever things were requisite for making bridges, and for barring and stopping up havens' mouths with stakes, posts, and other means, he commanded to be made ready.

Supplies

"Moreover not far from Neiuport haven, he had caused a great pile of wooden faggots to be laid, and other furniture to be brought for the rearing up of a mount. The most part of his ships contained two ovens a piece to bake bread in, with a great number of sadles, bridles, and other apparel for horses. They had horses likewise, which after their landing should serve to convey, and draw engines, field-pieces, and other warlike provisions (47)."

The Duke of Parma assembled quite an army in the Low Countries, ready to join up with the Armada: "Near to Neiuport he had assembled an army, over which he had ordained Camillo de Monte to be camp-master. This army consisted of 30 bands or ensigns of Italians, 10 bands of Walloons, eight of Scots, and eight of Burgundians, amounting to 56 bands, every band containing a hundred persons. Near to Dixmud there were mustered 80 bands of Dutch men, 60 of Spaniards, six of high Germans, and seven bands of English fugitives, under the conduct of Sir William Stanley, an English knight.

Parma's army

"In the suburbs of Cortreight there were 4,000 horsemen ready together with their horses. And at Waten there were 900 horses, with the troop of the Marquis del Gwasto, Captain General of the horsemen (48)."

Pope Sixtus V issued thousands of indulgences for the benefit of the invaders' souls: "Likewise Pope Sixtus V for the setting forth of the expedition, as they used to do against Turks and infidels, published a Cruzado, with most ample indulgences

Help from the Pope

61

Opposite Ambassadors from the Netherlands seek Elizabeth's aid against their Spanish overlords

which were printed in great numbers. These vain bulls the English and Dutchmen derided, saying that the Devil at all passages lay in ambush like a thief, no whit regarding such

Rope-making for the English fleet in the dockyards of Plymouth

letters of safe conduct (49)."

Philip wrote to the Duke of Parma, giving him his orders. *Philip's orders*
The Duke was to cross his army over the Channel as soon as *to Parma*

A dockyard metal worker employed by the English fleet

possible. "The Armada will anchor at Margate Point, having first sent notice to you at Dunkirk, Neiuport, or the Sluys, of his approach. When you see the passage assured by the arrival of the fleet at Margate, or at the mouth of the Thames, you will, if the weather permits, instantly cross with the whole army in the boats which you will have ready . . . You will see the danger of any delay, the Armada being there and you behindhand.

The Duke of Parma who commanded the Spanish army in the Low Countries

Philip II hears news of the Armada's progress

Until your passage is effected it will have no harbour for shelter, whereas when you have crossed over, it will have the safe and spacious River Thames. Otherwise, it will be at the mercy of the weather.

"You must not forget that the forces collected, and the vast money responsibility incurred, make it extremely difficult for such an expedition to be got together again if they escape us this time . . . Obstacles and divisions which may arise (and certainly will do so) next summer force us to undertake the enterprise this year, or else fail altogether (50)."

The provinces of Holland and Zeeland made their own preparations for defence against the Armada, and what might

happen: "But because the Spanish ships were described to them
to be so huge, they relied partly upon the shallow and dangerous
seas all along their coasts. And so they stood most in doubt of
the Duke of Parma's small flat-bottomed ships. But they had
all their ships of war to the number of 90 and above, ready for
all occasions. The greater part were of a small tonnage, as being
more meet to sail on their rivers and shallow seas. And with
these ships they besieged all the havens in Flanders, beginning
at the mouth of the Scheld, or from the town of Lillo, and
holding on to Gravelines and almost to Calais, and fortified
all their sea towns with strong garrisons (51)."

As Hakluyt explains, the Dutch were so well prepared – and
the morale and training of their men so high – that they were
able to blockade the Duke of Parma in his Flemish ports:
"Against the Spanish fleet's arrival, they had provided 25 or 30
good ships, putting them under Admiral Lonck, whom they
commanded to join with the Lord Henry Seymour lying between
Dover and Calais. And when these ships – of which the greater
part besieged the haven of Dunkirk – were driven by tempest
into Zeeland, Justin of Nassau, the Admiral of Zeeland, supplied
that squadron with 35 ships, being of no great size, but excellently
furnished with guns, mariners and soldiers in great abundance,
and especially with 1,200 brave musketeers, having been
accustomed to sea fights, and being chosen out of all their
companies for the same purpose. And so the said Justin of
Nassau kept such diligent ward in that station that the Duke of
Parma could not issue forth with his navy into the sea out of
any part of Flanders (52)."

7 Spain's New Grand Admiral

IN FEBRUARY, 1588, the Marquis of Santa Cruz fell seriously ill. After years of active service and high command, his health had been broken. Worsening relations with King Philip had not helped. Philip saw that the Marquis was close to death, and took the opportunity of appointing a new Grand Admiral of the Armada. His choice was the Duke of Medina Sidonia, who had defended Cadiz against Drake's raid the year before.

Philip wrote: "Dear Duke and Cousin: I have decided to confer on you the office of my Captain General of the Ocean Sea. Your first action will be to take charge of the Armada which I have ordered to assemble in Lisbon. And as speed is particularly important, if within eight or ten days you find that you are able to set out with the galleons provided with their full complement of sailors and soldiers, I charge you to embark and proceed straight to the mouth of the river of Lisbon without loss of time (53)."

The unlucky Duke was appalled by this sudden and un- *The unlucky* expected news. He had little naval experience, and no desire at *Duke* all to command a fleet – let alone the Armada by which Philip set so much store. He at once wrote to the King's secretary a long letter, imploring to be excused:

"I first humbly thank his Majesty for having thought of me for so great a task, and I wish I possessed the talents and strength necessary for it. But, sir, I have not health for the sea, for I know by the small experience that I have had afloat that I soon become seasick, and have many humours [sicknesses]. Besides this, your worship knows, as I have often told you

67

verbally and in writing, that I am in great need, so much so that when I have had to go to Madrid I have been obliged to borrow money for the journey. My house owes 900,000 ducats, and I am therefore quite unable to accept the command. I have not a single real [coin] I can spend on the expedition.

"Apart from this, neither my conscience nor my duty will allow me to take this service upon me. The force is so great, and the undertaking so important, that it would not be right for a person like myself, possessing no experience of seafaring or of war, to take charge of it. So, sir, in the interest of his Majesty's service, and for the love I bear him, I submit to you, for communication to him, that I possess neither aptitude, ability, health, nor fortune, for the expedition (54)."

Philip determined

But King Philip was not to be put off: "I have permitted my decision to be made public here, and written to Portugal and Flanders. I charge you to do this, and also to acquaint yourself fully with the object of this enterprise – how it is to be conducted, and the manner in which your plans may be co-ordinated with those of the Duke of Parma, my nephew. Very special instructions and advices will reach you in Lisbon, dealing with what you should do there . . .

"Prepare and steel yourself to the performance of this service in the manner I expect from you. Help me also to do this service for God, since this is my chief aim in what I have undertaken. Advise me quickly of all that you have done. I can but think that this letter will find you nearer Lisbon than San Lucar, since the confidence I place in you forces you to do no less (55)."

Philip bombarded his new Grand Admiral with reams of instructions and advice. One of the problems was recruiting seamen for what was obviously going to be a major sea battle. Philip made a suggestion to Medina Sidonia: "The general opinion here lately has been that it would be as well to spread the report that the galleons are bound for the Indies, so as the more easily to recruit the necessary men, particularly seamen. Now, however it may be that recruits will respond more readily to the call of the Armada, than to that of the Indies, yet, as far as the sailors are concerned, I feel it would be well that they should believe the report of the Indies (56)."

Unhappily, Medina Sidonia read the daily messages from his King, telling him to "keep an eye on all your administrative officers," and saying how much trust he put in "your excellent management and vigilance." Another royal letter read: "Keep me informed of all you do, and of all that happens. These are all the instructions which for the time being it occurs to me to give to you (57)."

Wearily, Medina Sidonia hoisted his flag in the *San Martin*, a ship of 1,000 tons. Its crew was 117 sailors and 300 soldiers, and its armaments 48 guns. Altogether, the Duke had about 130 ships under his command, and a total force of 29,000 men, including 2,000 convicts working as rowers in the galleasses and galleys.

Once he had accepted his burden of duty, Medina Sidonia *Taking* busied himself in the details of naval administration. With his *command* personal staff of 22 gentlemen and 50 servants he studied the supplies and equipment of the fleet, and the condition of the seamen. On a personal tour of inspection, he found many things lacking. Some of the seamen's pay was very much in arrears, and some of them had actually died of want, "like two of the best pilots did yesterday. I entreat Your Majesty to pay them. Duarte has produced the clothing contracts for the infantry, galleass and galley chain-gangs, which seem good as to price and credit terms, if Your Majesty would confirm it (58)."

At length, as King Philip had instructed him, the Duke *Armada meets* brought the great fleet out of Lisbon and up the Portuguese *a tempest* coast. But he ran into a great storm, and his fleet was scattered, forcing him to regroup his forces at the port of Corunna:

"As they were sailing along, there arose such a mighty tempest, that the whole fleet was dispersed, so that when the Duke returned to his company, he could not see above 80 ships in all, to which the residue by little and little joined themselves, except eight which had their masts blown overboard. One of the four galleys of Portugal barely escaped, retiring herself into the haven. The other three were upon the coast of Bayonne in France, by the assistance and courage of one David Gwyn, an English captive . . . one of the three was first overcome, which conquered the two other, with the slaughter of their governors

69

Overleaf The Spanish were feared and hated by their Dutch subjects. In 1576 many of the Protestant people of Antwerp were massacred by the Spaniards

NTORFF.

and soldiers, and among the rest of Don Diego de Mandrana with sundry others. And so those slaves arrived in France with the three galleys, and set themselves at liberty (59)."

In the meantime, Medina Sidonia wrote again to King Philip, urging him to reconsider the whole expedition, and once more asking to be relieved of his command.

But Philip replied: "His Majesty continues firm in his resolution to carry forward the task . . . our efforts against England are but the will of God in man's hands, for the enterprise against heretic England is least of all influenced by motives of personal interest or royal aggrandizement, the chief consideration being to defend God's cause. To abandon our purpose now would be to the benefit of the Protestant horde. The enemies of the Catholic religion would interpret the damage inflicted by the storm as authority for their heresies, twisting in their favour God's tolerance (60)."

In the same letter, Philip reminded Medina Sidonia of all the advantages Spain had over England: "Of the enemy's ships, some are old; others small, and inferior to ours in strength and general excellence. Do not forget the numerical superiority of our crews, and the long experience enjoyed by many of them. The enemy's crews, on the other hand, consist of novices, drawn from the common people – a tumultuous crowd, lacking military discipline.

"Remember, too, that at this juncture England stands stripped of allies. Had aid come from France, it might have been formidable. But they are in no condition there to send help, owing to their internal feuds. The rebels in Holland and Zeeland care more for their own interests. The German Protestants are at most only able to create some slight diversion, which cannot avert the blows which the Armada will deliver. The Danish King, the enemy's most powerful supporter, who could have reinforced the English fleet, is dead, and that news has caused hope to fade . . .

"As for the King of Scotland, no help can be looked for from him, for the blood of his beheaded mother [Mary Queen of Scots, executed by Queen Elizabeth] is not yet congealed. One might rather expect that the Scottish forces would themselves move to attack the English from their side. The Armada will put out for England at the earliest opportunity (61)."

Philip was annoyed to hear that the Armada had put in at Corunna. He sent daily orders to Medina Sidonia to take to sea again: "The navy having refreshed themselves at the Groine, and receiving daily orders from the King to hasten their journey, hoisted up sails the 11th day of July. Holding on their course till the 19th of the same month, they came to the mouth of the English Channel. From there, they dispatched certain of their small ships to the Duke of Parma. At the same time the Spanish fleet was sighted by an English pinnace, whose captain was Mr. Thomas Fleming (62)."

On to the Channel

8 The Armada Sighted

WHILE CAPTAIN FLEMING raced his pinnace back to Plymouth with news of the Armada, other news was already reaching London. An English spy had intercepted a letter from Lisbon which showed that the invasion attempt was imminent: "All things are embarked, even the mules that must draw the artillery. On pain of death, no man may go ashore; we only tarry for a fair wind to go to sea. There is given every day 22,000 rations of victual to the people for sea and land . . . This only to Spaniards, besides strangers (63)."

Howard wrote to Lord Burghley from Plymouth: "God send us the happiness to meet with them before our men on the land discover them, for I fear me a little sight of the enemy will fear the land men much (64)."

The Lord Admiral was still very worried about the lack of victuals, which meant that many ships could not leave port to seek the enemy out. On 22nd June he wrote to the Council: "My Lords, our victuals are not yet come, but we hope shortly to hear of them if this wind continue 40 hours, or else we cannot tell what to think of them, or what should become of them; and yet we have sent three or four pinnaces to seek them out. If they come not, our extremity will be very great, for our victuals ended the 15th of this month. *Lack of victuals*

"If Mr. Darell had not very carefully provided us with 14 days' victuals, and again with four or five days' more, which now he has provided, we would have been in some great extremity. Mr. Hawkins has disbursed money for all that, and for many other charges Sir Francis Drake has likewise disbursed some.

75

Opposite Plymouth quayside and castle as Drake would have known it

"And so, to avoid the danger and inconvenience that may follow, it would do very well if her Majesty would send five or six thousand pounds hither, for it is likely we shall stand in great need of it."

And he added: "I pray your Lordships to pardon me that I may remind you to move her Majesty that she may have an especial care to draw ten or twelve thousand men about her own person, that may not be men unpractised (65)."

Sickness and storms

Sickness and bad weather added to Howard's problems: "Several men have fallen sick, and thousands seek to be discharged, and other pressed in their stead. This has been an infinite charge with great trouble to us, the army being so great as it is, the ships so many in number, and the weather so extreme foul as it has been; whereby great charges have risen and daily do. And yet I protest before God we have been more careful of her Majesty's charges than of our own lives (66)."

Spies

About this time, some spies came back to London with fresh reports from the coast of Spain. They had heard that the Armada had been scattered by storms, and forced to shelter in the port of Corunna. They "were of opinion that the navy being of late dispersed, and tossed up and down the open sea, were by no means able to perform their intended voyage. Moreover, the Lord Charles Howard, Lord High Admiral of England, had received letters from the Court, signifying to him that her Majesty was advised that the Spanish fleet would not come forth, nor was to be any longer expected, and so that, on her Majesty's orders, he must send back four of her tallest and strongest ships to Chatham (67)." Howard was furious. Not only had the Council kept him short of rations, and told him to demobilize part of his force—now they sought to take away his battleships.

A game of bowls

But no sooner had he received these orders than he heard Captain Fleming's breathless news that the Armada was approaching the English Channel. Fleming found Howard, Drake, and some of the other officers in the middle of a game of bowls on the grassy slopes of Plymouth Hoe. Drake said, "We have time to finish the game and beat the Spaniards too." Whether the game of bowls was finished we do not know.

One can imagine Howard's feelings as he heard the news:

"With all speed and diligence possible he warped his ships, and caused his mariners and soldiers to come on board, and that with great trouble and difficulty, so that the Lord Admiral himself was forced to lie without in the road [anchorage] with six ships only all that night, after which many others came forth of the haven (68)."

Howard sights the Armada

Howard had only 24 hours to wait before sighting the Armada for himself: "The very next day being the 20th of July about high noon, the Spanish fleet was sighted by the English. With a south-west wind it came sailing along, and passed by Plymouth (69)."

An opportunity missed

Some Spanish experts felt that the Armada should have struck at Plymouth. For it was "the most convenient port of all others, where they might with greater security have been given news of the English forces, and how the commons of the land stood affected, and might have stirred up some mutiny, so that from here they should have bent all their strength, and the Duke of Parma might more easily have conveyed his ships.

"But this they were prohibited to do by the King and his council, and were expressly commanded to unite themselves to the soldiers and ships of the said Duke of Parma, and so bring their purpose to effect. This was thought to be the most easy and direct course, for they all imagined that the English and Dutchmen would be utterly daunted and dismayed thereat, and would all retire to their own province and port for the defence thereof. And, transporting the army of the Duke under the protection of their huge navy, they might invade England (70)."

Many Spanish officers "found fault that they were bound to so strict directions and instructions, because that in such a case many particular accidents ought to concur and to be respected at one and the same instant, that is to say, the opportunity of the wind, weather, time, tide, and ebb, wherein they might sail from Flanders to England. Often too the darkness and light, the situation of places, the depths and shoals were to be considered: all of which especially depended upon the convenience of the winds, and were so much the more dangerous (71)."

But King Philip had commanded the Armada to anchor "near to, or about Calais, whither the Duke of Parma was to resort with his ships and all his warlike provision, and while the

77

Overleaf Sir Francis Drake was in the middle of a game of bowls when he heard that the Spanish fleet had been sighted

English and Spanish great ships were in the midst of their conflict, to pass by, and land his soldiers upon the Downs (72)."

Philip wants London

The Spanish King wanted his Armada to make for the River Thames, and "to have passed with small ships up to London, supposing that they might easily win that rich and flourishing City, which was meanly fortified and inhabited with citizens not used to wars, who durst not withstand their first encounter. He hoped also to find many rebels against her Majesty, and Popish Catholics, or some favourers of the Scottish Queen – who was not long before most justly beheaded – who might be instruments of sedition (73)."

But things were not to turn out as the Spanish King had expected. For as the Armada came into the Channel, Medina Sidonia was amazed to see the English fleet at his rear. Lord Howard had managed to slip his fleet quickly out of Plymouth, and seized the advantage of the wind.

The Armada now had to look to its defence.

The *Ark Royal*, flag-ship of Queen Elizabeth's navy

9 The Battle in the Channel

THE ENGLISH FLEET had the advantage of the wind over the *English* Armada. But many of the officers and men were dismayed to see *dismay* its sheer size. The lookouts on the topmasts gave up trying to count the number of ships. As Drake watched, the Armada began to take up its battle formation – the ominous crescent. The ships were so thick in the middle of the crescent that no one but a madman would have sought to attack there: but on the wings of the crescent stood the most powerful galleons in the entire Armada. A direct attack on its flanks could be equally dangerous.

Howard decided to come within range of the Armada, and *Howard's* concentrate on gunfire, rather than on close engagement. *tactics* Richard Hakluyt takes up the story. The "English ships approached within musket shot of the Spanish. At that time the Lord Charles Howard most hotly and valiantly discharged his ordnance upon the Spanish Vice-Admiral. Seeing the nimbleness of the English ships in discharging upon the enemy on all sides, the Spanish gathered themselves close into the form of a half moon, and slackened their sails, lest they should leave any of their company behind. And while they were proceeding on in this manner, one of their great galleasses was so furiously battered with shot, that the whole navy was forced to come up rounder together for its safety. And so it came to pass that the principal galleon of Seville (in which Don Pedro de Valdez, Vasques de Silva, Alonzo de Sayas, and other noblemen were embarked) falling foul of another ship, had her foremast broken, and so was not able to keep up with the Spanish fleet. Neither

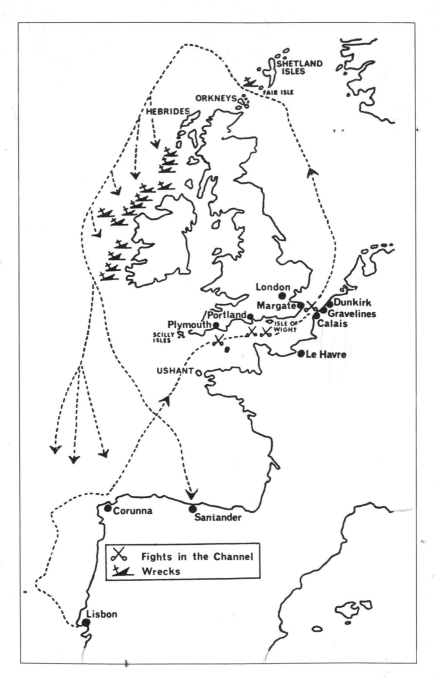

The course of the Spanish Armada

would the said fleet stay to succour it, but left the distressed galleon behind.

"The Lord Admiral of England when he saw this ship of Valdez, and though she had been emptied of Mariners and soldiers, took with him as many ships as he could, and passed by it, that he might not lose sight of the Spanish fleet that night . . . The Lord Admiral all that night following the Spanish lantern instead of the English, found himself in the morning to be in the midst of his enemy's fleet, but when he perceived it, he cleanly conveyed himself out of that great danger (74)."

And so the capture of Valdez's ship fell to Sir Francis Drake. *Drake makes* Next day, "Sir Francis Drake spied Valdez's ship whereunto *a capture* he sent forth his pinnace. Being told that Valdez himself was there, and 450 persons with him, he sent him word that he should yield himself. Valdez for his honour's sake caused certain conditions to be put to Drake: who answered Valdez that he was not now at leisure to make any long parley, but if he would yield himself, he should find him friendly and tractable . . .

"Upon which answer Valdez and his company . . . yielded themselves, and found him very favourable to them. Then Valdez with 40 or 50 noblemen and gentlemen attached to him, came on board Sir Francis Drake's ship. The residue of his company were carried to Plymouth, where they were detained a year and a half for their ransom (75)."

Valdez gave Drake information about the Armada. He "began *Valdez* to tell Drake the forces of all the Spanish fleet, and how four mighty galleys were separated by tempest from them: and also how they were determined first to have put into Plymouth haven, not expecting to be repelled by the English ships . . . They marvelled much how the Englishmen in their small ships dared approach within musket shot of the Spaniards' mighty wooden castles, gathering the wind of them with many other such attempts (76)."

Howard and the English commanders greatly overestimated *Harrying the* the size of the Armada. Rather than engage in a head-on fight *Spanish* with the great crescent formation, they began to attack its wings, in the hope of harrying and dispersing the great formation. The English sailors were much more familiar with the tricky winds

83

Overleaf The two fleets tracking each other up the English Channel

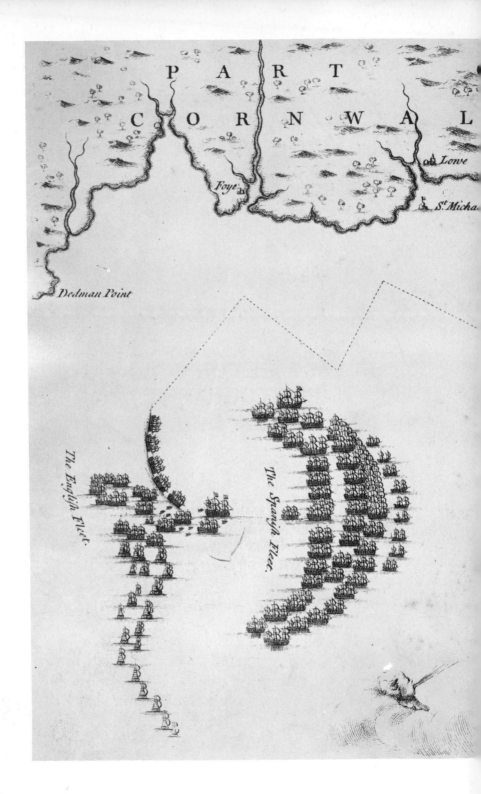

P A R T

C O R N W A L

Lowe

Foye

St Micha

Dedman Point

The English Fleet.

The Spanish Fleet.

Saltash

Plymouth

Milbrook

Mount Edgcomb

Causon

Shagstone Point

Shagstone

Menstone

Eddy Stone

and cross-currents of the English Channel. This was why the Spanish were allowed to go so far up the Channel. It was a dangerous policy: no one knew whether the Spanish might suddenly try to make a landing – perhaps at Weymouth, perhaps at the Isle of Wight, or elsewhere on the south coast.

But by degrees, the faster English ships were able to claim isolated victories. As Hakluyt reported: "The same day was set on fire one of the greatest ships [the *San Salvador*] which contained great store of gunpowder and other warlike provisions. The upper part only of this ship was burnt, and all persons therein contained – except a very few – were consumed with fire ... It was taken by the English, and brought into England with a number of miserable burnt and scorched Spaniards. Yet the gunpowder, to the great admiration of all men, remained whole and unconsumed (77)."

The San Salvador   Howard sent his nephew, Lord Thomas Howard of the *Golden Lion*, to take possession of the vessel, the *San Salvador*. "All the superstructure of the ship had been wrecked by fire, and there were still aboard fifty men ... who had been burned by the gunpowder and some languished, not yet dead, and the stench was so overpowering and the ship everywhere so filthy that Howard very soon left, forbidding his soldiers to board her." The wreck was towed in to Weymouth (78).

Battle of Portland   A great crisis appeared as the Armada approached Portland: "The navy being come over against Portland, the wind began to turn northerly, so that the Spaniards had a fortunate and fit gale to invade the English. But the Englishmen having lesser and nimbler ships, recovered again the vantage of the wind from the Spaniards, at which the Spaniards seemed to be more incensed to fight than before.

"But when the English fleet had ... from morning to night beaten and battered them with all their shot both great and small, the Spaniards united themselves and gathered their whole fleet close together into a roundel, so that it was apparent that they meant not as yet to invade others, but only to defend themselves and make haste to the place [near] Dunkirk, that they might join forces with the Duke of Parma, who was determined to have proceeded secretly with his small ships under the shadow and protection of the great ones, and so had intended circumspectly to perform the whole expedition. This was the most furious and bloody skirmish of all (79)."

After the Battle of Portland, more ships were brought from the south coast ports to reinforce Howard's fleet: "The English navy in the meanwhile increased. Out of all havens of the realm resorted ships and men, for they all with one accord came flocking thither as to a set of field, where immortal fame and glory was to be attained, and faithful service to be performed to their prince and country . . .(80)"

Soon the wind dropped, and the English ships found themselves almost becalmed. But the Spanish galleasses were equipped with oars, and so had the advantage. Since "the sea was calm, and no wind stirring, the fight was only between the four great galleasses and the English ships, which being rowed with oars, had great advantage of the said English ships. The English discharged their chain-shot to cut asunder the cables and cordage of the galleasses, with many other such stratagems. They were now forced to send their men on land for a new supply of gunpowder, whereof they were in great scarcity, as they had so freely spent the greater part in the former conflicts (81)."

But still the Armada was at sea. Where would the Spanish try to put their armies ashore? The Isle of Wight seemed the next most vulnerable point, and troops were rapidly brought to defend the Island, many of them from the county of Kent. Much depended on the outcome of the next deadly clash between the rival fleets. Hakluyt paid tribute to the Armada's good sailing order: "The Spaniards in their sailing observed very diligent and good order, sailing three and four, and sometimes more ships in a rank, and following close up one after another, and the stronger and greater ships protecting the lesser.

"The 25th of July, when the Spaniards were come over against the Isle of Wight, the Lord Admiral of England being accompanied with his best ships . . . with great valour and dreadful thundering of shot, found the Spanish Admiral in the very midst of all his fleet. When the Spaniard perceived this, being assisted with his strongest ships, he came forth and entered a terrible combat with the English: for they bestowed on each other

87

Overleaf The *Ark Royal* closes with one of the Spanish galleons

The confusion of battle: on the left a Spanish ship is in flames ignited by
one of the deadly English fire-ships

broadsides, and mutually discharged all their ordnance, being
within 100 or 120 yards of one another.

"At length the Spaniards hoisted up their sails, and again
gathered themselves up close into the form of a roundel. Meanwhile Captain Frobisher had engaged himself in a most dangerous
conflict. Coming to succour him, the Lord Admiral found that
he had valiantly and discreetly behaved himself, and had wisely
and in good time given over the fight, because that after so great
a battery he had sustained no damage.

"For which the day following, being the 26th of July, the Lord
Admiral rewarded him with the order of knighthood, together
with the Lord Thomas Howard, the Lord Sheffield, Mr. John
Hawkins and others (82)."

After the battle off the Isle of Wight, the Armada – now feeling the effects of the devastating English gunnery – cruised up the Channel, heading for the Dover–Calais straits. The Duke of Medina Sidonia planned to unite his fleet with that of the Duke of Parma and his army of invasion. But he did not realize that Parma was blockaded in his ports in the Low Countries by the Dutch fleet:

"The 27th of July, the Spaniards about sunset were come over against Dover, and rode at anchor within sight of Calais, intending to hold on for Dunkirk, expecting there to join with the Duke of Parma's forces, without which they were able to do little or nothing.

"Likewise the English fleet following up hard upon them, anchored just by them within culverin shot. And here the Lord Henry Seymour united himself with the Lord Admiral with his fleet of 30 ships which rode before the mouth of the Thames.

"As the Spanish navy therefore lay at anchor, the Duke of Medina sent certain messengers to the Duke of Parma . . .

"Upon Tuesday, 30th of July, about high noon, he came to Dunkirk, when all the Spanish fleet was now passed by. Neither durst any of his ships in the meantime come forth to assist the Spanish fleet for fear of 35 warlike ships of Holland and Zeeland, which kept watch and ward under the conduct of the Admiral Justin of Nassau."

His ships "were furnished with most cunning mariners and experienced soldiers, among which were 1,200 musketeers, whom the States had chosen out of all their garrisons, and whom they knew to be experienced in seafights.

"This navy was especially charged not to allow any ship to come out of the haven, nor to permit any zabraes, patches or other small vessels of the Spanish fleet . . . The greater ships were not to be feared by reason of the shallow sea in that place . . .

"Moreover, the ships of Holland and Zeeland stood continually in their sight, threatening shot and powder . . . for fear of which the mariners and seamen secretly withdrew themselves both day and night, in case the Duke of Parma's soldiers should compel them to go on board, and break through the Hollanders' fleet, which all of them judged to be impossible by reason of the

Overleaf Lord Howard knights the captains of the English ships on board the *Ark Royal* after the Spanish defeat

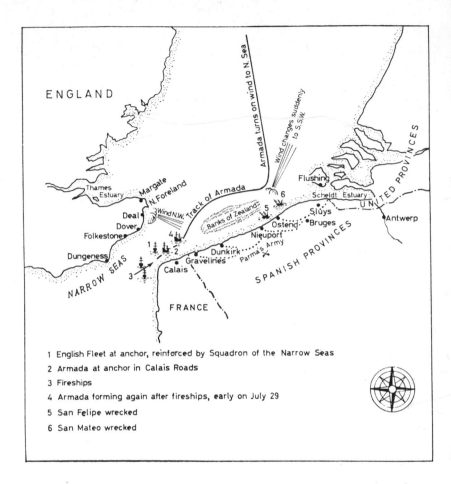

The labels within the map:

ENGLAND

Armada turns on wind to N. Sea

Wind changes suddenly to S.S.W.

Flushing

Thames Estuary

Margate

N. Foreland

Track of Armada

Scheldt Estuary

UNITED PROVINCES

Deal

Dover

Folkestone

Wind N.W.

Banks of Zealand

6

5

Sluys

Ostend

Bruges

Antwerp

Nieuport

Dungeness

Dunkirk

Parma's Army

SPANISH PROVINCES

NARROW SEAS

Gravelines

Calais

FRANCE

1 English Fleet at anchor, reinforced by Squadron of the Narrow Seas
2 Armada at anchor in Calais Roads
3 Fireships
4 Armada forming again after fireships, early on July 29
5 San Felipe wrecked
6 San Mateo wrecked

The position of the fleets at the Battle of Gravelines

straightness of the haven (83)."

Fire ships   While Medina Sidonia held his fleet between Gravelines and Calais, trying to get news of the Duke of Parma, Lord Howard seized his chance. He took eight of his oldest ships and turned them into terrible floating incendiaries. Fearful rumours began to reach the Spanish commanders of the Armada. The famous Italian engineer Federico Giambelli was reputed to be in England at this time – and he was known for his work three years before in equipping ships as immense bombs, detonated by flintlock

94

devices operated by clockwork.

Howard emptied the ships "of all things which seemed to be of value, filled them with gunpowder, pitch, brimstone, and with other combustible and fiery matter; and charging all their ordnance with powder, bullets, and stones, he sent the ships on the 28th of July, being Sunday, about two o'clock after midnight, with the wind and tide, against the Spanish fleet . . .

"When they had proceeded a good space, they were abandoned by the pilots, set on fire, and directly carried upon the King of Spain's navy. This fire in the dead of the night put the Spaniards into such a perplexity and horror . . . that cutting the cables on which their anchors were fastened, and hoisting up their sails, they took themselves very confusedly to the open sea.

"In this sudden confusion the principal and greatest of the four galleasses fell foul of another ship, and lost her rudder. And when she could not be steered any longer, she was by the force of the tide cast into a certain shoal on the shore of Calais, where she was immediately assaulted by divers English pinnaces (84)."

Even after the victory of Gravelines at the end of July, the English were still worried. After all, the Duke of Parma's army was still only a few miles away on the other side of the English Channel. A French fleet under the Duke of Guise could easily bring them over on a single tide.

Victory of Gravelines

At the end of this great day Howard wrote to Walsingham: "We have chased them in fight until this evening late, and distressed them much, but their fleet consists of mighty ships and great strength. Yet we doubt not, by God's good assistance, to oppress them . . . Their force is wonderful great and strong, and yet we pluck their feathers by little and little. I pray to God that the powers on the land be strong enough to answer so present a force (85)."

Drake wrote: "God has given us so good a day in forcing the enemy so far to leeward, as I hope in God the Prince of Parma and the Duke of Sidonia shall not shake hands this few days. And whenever they shall meet, I believe neither of them will greatly rejoice of this day's service . . . I assure your Honour this day's service has much appalled the enemy (86)."

95

Overleaf The Spanish fleet anchored off Calais is attacked by fireships from the English fleet

DIEU・E

According to Hakluyt, Sir Francis Drake had been lucky to escape with his life: "Sir Francis Drake's ship was pierced with shot above forty times, and his very cabin was twice shot through. And about the conclusion of the fight, the bed of a certain gentleman lying weary thereupon, was taken quite from under him with the force of a bullet. Likewise, when the Earl of Northumberland and Sir Charles Blunt were at dinner, the bullet of a demi-culverin broke through the middle of their cabin, touched their feet, and struck down two of the standers-by (87)."

At Gravelines the Armada had suffered much heavier losses than the English: "The Spaniards that day sustained great loss and damage, having many of their ships shot through and through. They discharged a great store of ordnance against the English, who indeed sustained some hindrance, but not comparable to the Spaniards' loss: for they lost not one ship or person... (88)"

At the end of July, Queen Elizabeth was demanding from London why Howard was not trying to board more of the Spanish ships: "What causes are there why the Spanish navy has not been boarded by the Queen's ships? And though some of the ships of Spain may be thought too huge to be boarded by the English, yet some of the Queen's ships are thought very able to have boarded some of the meaner ships of the Spanish navy (89)."

Writing afterwards, Sir Walter Raleigh praised Howard for his tactics. He was right to use his guns at a distance, rather than to try and grapple with the enemy at close quarters: "There is more belonging to a good man of war, upon the waters, than great daring . . . There is a great deal of difference between fighting loose or at large, and grappling. The guns of a slow ship pierce as well, and make as great holes, as those in a swift. To clap ships together, without consideration, belongs rather to a madman than to a man of war (90)."

Raleigh added, "The Spaniards had an army aboard them, and he [Howard] had none. They had more ships than he had, and of higher building and charging . . . Had he entangled himself with those great and powerful vessels, he would have greatly endangered this Kingdom of England. For 20 men upon the defences are equal to 100 that board and enter (91)."

10 Towards Victory

AT THE BEGINNING of August, while the fleets were in the Channel, Elizabeth went down to Tilbury on the Thames, to review her troops under the command of the Earl of Leicester. In a famous speech, she promised to fight at the head of her armies if the Spaniards should dare set foot on English soil: *Elizabeth at Tilbury*

"My loving people, we have been persuaded by some that are careful of our safety, to take heed how we commit ourselves to armed multitudes, for fear of treachery. But I assure you, I do not desire to live to distrust my faithful and loving people. Let tyrants fear. I have always so behaved myself that, under God, I have placed my chiefest strength and safeguard in the loyal hearts and goodwill of my subjects; and therefore I am come amongst you, as you see, at this time – not for my recreation and disport – but being resolved, in the midst and heat of the battle, to live or die amongst you all, to lay down for my God, and for my kingdom, and for my people, my honour and my blood, even in the dust.

"I know I have the body of a weak and feeble woman, but I have the heart and stomach of a king, and of a king of England too, and think foul scorn that Parma or Spain, or any prince of Europe should dare to invade the borders of my realm; to which, rather than any dishonour shall grow by me, I myself will take up arms. I myself will be your general, judge, and rewarder of every one of your virtues in the field (92)." *"The heart and stomach of a king"*

Soon after she had reviewed the troops at Tilbury, a message came that the Duke of Parma was about to launch his invasion: "This day, at noon, her Majesty, dining with the Lord Steward in his tent, was told by report from Sir Thomas Morgan, *Elizabeth confident*

Elizabeth addresses her troops at Tilbury, on the River Thames near London

newly arrived from the Hague, that the Duke of Parma was determined to come out this high tide, and had arranged this with Medina Sidonia at Calais. But her Majesty, after considering the report, was not too much alarmed by it." She had "a conceit, that in honour she could not return, in case there were any likelihood that the enemy would attempt anything . . . This place breedeth courage (93)."

While Elizabeth anxiously waited at Tilbury for news of the battle in the Channel, the English fleet was working hard to try and pick off the Spanish stragglers. Many had suffered so badly from gunshot that they foundered of their own accord: "The Spanish ships were so battered with English shot, that that very night and the day following, two or three of them sunk right down. Among the rest a certain great ship of Biscay, which Captain Crosse assaulted, perished even in the time of the conflict, so that very few therein escaped drowning." *Attacking stragglers*

The Captain "reported that the governors of the same ship slew one another [for] one of them which would have yielded the ship was suddenly slain. The brother of the slain party in revenge of his death slew the murderer, and in the meanwhile the ship sunk.

"The same night two Portuguese galleons of seven or eight hundred tons apiece, to wit the *Saint Philip* and the *Saint Matthew*, were abandoned by the Spanish fleet, for they were so torn with shot that the water entered into them on all sides. In the galleon of *Saint Philip* was Francis de Toledo, brother of the Count de Orgas, who was Colonel over two and thirty bands: besides other gentlemen, who seeing their mast broken with shot shaped their course . . . for the coast of Flanders (94)."

One Spanish captain was too proud to accept help from Medina Sidonia. But he was to pay the price: "In the other galleon, called the *Saint Matthew*, was embarked Don Diego Pimentelli, another camp-master and colonel of 32 bands, being brother of the Marquis of Tamnares, with many other gentlemen and captains. Their ship was not very great, but exceeding strong, for a great number of bullets which had battered her, there were scarce 20 wherewith she was pierced or hurt: her upper work was of force sufficient to bear off a musket shot. *The proud Spaniard*

"This ship was shot through and pierced in the fight before

101

Gravelines, so that the leakage of the water could not be stopped. Whereupon the Duke of Medina sent his great skiff to the governor thereof, that he might save himself and the principal persons that were in his ship. But he, with high courage, refused to do, wherefore the Duke charged him to sail next to himself. The night following he could not perform this, by reasons of the great abundance of water which entered his ship on all sides. To avoid this, and to save his ship from sinking, he caused 50 men continually to labour at the pump, though it were to small purpose.

"Seeing himself thus forsaken and separated from his Admiral, he did what he could to attain the coast of Flanders: where, being spied by four or five men of war, stationed on the same coast, he was admonished to yield himself to them. This he refused to do, and was strongly assaulted by them altogether, and his ship being pierced with many bullets, was brought into far worse case than before, and 40 of his soldiers were slain. By this extremity he was forced at length to yield himself to Peter Banderduess and other captains, who brought him and his ship into Zeeland, with that other ship also mentioned. And both of them, immediately after the greater and better part of their goods were unladen, sunk right down.

"For the memory of this exploit, Captain Banderduess caused the banner of one of these ships to be set up in the great Church of Leyden in Holland, which was so long that being fastened to the very roof, it reached down to the ground (95)."

The Armada had been badly shaken. But still the English ships were too few and too small to think of direct assault.

"There were many excellent and warlike ships in the English fleet, yet scarce were there 22 or 23 among them all which matched 90 of the Spanish ships in size, or could conveniently assault them. Wherefore the English ships, using the prerogative of nimble steerage, whereby they could turn and wield themselves with the wind which way they wanted, came often very near the Spaniards, and charged them so sore, that now and then they were but a pike's length asunder. And so continually giving them one broadside after another, they discharged all their shot both great and small upon them, spending one whole day from morning till night in that violent kind of conflict, until such

Stragglers from the Spanish fleet were quickly picked off by the English

time as powder and bullets failed them.

"In regard of this want they thought it best not to pursue the Spaniards any longer, because they had many great advantages over the English, namely for the extraordinary size of their ships, and also because they were so nearly joined and kept together in so good array, that they could by no means be fought withal one to one. The English thought therefore, that they had right well acquitted themselves, in chasing the Spaniards first from Calais, and then from Dunkirk, and so hindered them from joining with the Duke of Parma's forces, and getting the wind of them, to have driven them from their own coasts (96)."

Howard short of supplies   Howard very soon found himself dangerously short of supplies, including powder and shot. And it was in his guns that he put all his trust. He was short of food, too. Hurriedly, he wrote to Walsingham: "I pray you to send with all speed as much as you can . . . As some of our ships are victualled but for a very short time, and my Lord Henry Seymour with his company not for one day, I pray you to dispatch away our victuals with all possible speed, because we know not whether we shall be forced to pursue the Spanish fleet (97)."

Armada in flight   Harried and pursued by the English fleet, the Armada was slowly but surely breaking up. The massive crescent formation had been smashed. The Duke of Medina Sidonia had sent repeated messages to the Duke of Parma to come out of the Low Countries, but to no avail. The English captains rejoiced to see that the Armada appeared to be in flight, moving up into the North Sea.

Howard "pursued the Spanish fleet until the second of August, because he thought they had set sail for Scotland. And although he followed them very near, yet he did not assault them any more, for want of powder and bullets . . . Upon the fourth of August, the wind arising, the Spaniards spread all their sails, taking themselves wholly to flight, and leaving Scotland on the left hand, made towards Norway, by which they sufficiently declared that their whole intent was to save themselves by flight, attempting for that purpose, with their battered and crazed ships, the most dangerous navigation of the Northern seas (98)."

North Sea dangers   Howard felt it was too dangerous to pursue the Armada at this time. The North Sea was rough and squally, and in any case

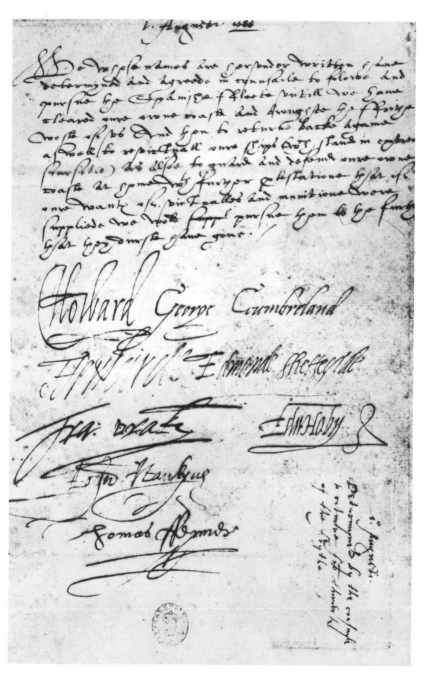

The resolution signed by the English naval commanders to pursue the
Spanish fleet after its defeat at Gravelines

he had almost run out of ammunition and other supplies. "The English seeing that they were now proceeded unto the latitude of 57 degrees, and being unwilling to share that danger in which the Spaniards plunged themselves, and because they lacked necessary supplies, especially powder and shot, returned back for England, leaving behind them certain pinnaces only, which they ordered to follow the Spaniards at a distance and to observe their course.

"And so it came to pass that the fourth of August, with great danger and industry, the English arrived at Harwich: for they had been tossed up and down with a mighty tempest for the space of two or three days together, which it is likely did great hurt to the Spanish fleet, being, as I said before, so maimed and battered (99)."

Pause at Harwich The English went ashore at Harwich, and "provided themselves forthwith with victuals, gunpowder, and other things expedient, that they might be ready at all times to engage the Spanish fleet, if it chanced any more to return. But being afterward more certainly informed of the Spaniards' course, they thought it best to leave them to those boisterous and uncouth Northern seas, and not there to hunt after them (100)."

In fact, Howard decided to leave part of his fleet at Harwich, under Lord Seymour and Lord Winter. The supplies he had repeatedly asked for were still in desperately short supply, and at a council of war held in the fleet he and his captains wrote a bitter letter of complaint to the Privy Council:

"We whose names are hereunder written have determined and agreed in council to follow and pursue the Spanish fleet until we have cleared our own coast and brought the Firth of Forth west of us; and then to return back again, as well to revictual our ships, which stand in extreme scarcity, as also to guard and defend our own coast at home. We further protest that, if our wants of victual and munition were supplied, we would pursue them to the furthest that they durst have gone (101)."

Fever scare To add to all his other worries, Howard was given news of a sudden fever in his fleet. He wrote to Lord Burghley on 10th August: "My good Lord, sickness and mortality begins wonderfully to grow amongst us; and it is a most pitiful sight to see, here at Margate, how the men, having no place to receive them here, die in the streets. I am driven myself, of force, to come a-land, to see them bestowed in some lodging; and the best I can get is barns and such outhouses; and the relief is small that I can provide for them here. It would grieve any man's heart to see them that have served so valiantly to die so miserably.

"The *Elizabeth Jonas*, which has done as well as ever any ship did in any service, has had a great infection in her from the beginning. Of the 500 men which she carried out, by the time we had been in Plymouth three weeks or a month, there were dead of them 200 and above. I was driven to set all the rest of her men ashore, to take out her ballast, and to make fires in her of wet broom, three or four days together; and so hoped thereby to have cleansed her of her infection; and thereupon got new men, very tall and able as ever I saw, and put them into her.

"Now the infection is broken out in greater extremity than ever it did before, and the men die and sicken faster than ever they did; and I am driven to send her to Chatham. We all think and judge that the infection remains in the pitch. Sir Roger Townshend, of all the men he brought out with him, has but one left alive, and my son Southwell likewise has many dead.

"It is probable that the like infection will grow throughout the most part of our fleet; for they have been so long at sea and have so little apparel, and so few places to provide them with such wants, and no money wherewith to buy it, for some have been – yea the most part – these eight months at sea.

"My Lord I would think it a marvellous good way that there were a £1,000 worth or 2,000 marks' worth of hose, doublets, shirts, shoes and suchlike, sent down; and I think your Lordship might use therein the Controller of the Navy and Waker, Mr. Hawkins' man, who would use all expedition for the providing and sending away of such things. For else, in very short time, I look to see most of the mariners go naked. Good my Lord, let mariners be pressed and sent down as soon as may be; and money to discharge those that be sick here; and so, in haste, I bid your Lordship farewell (102)."

The English tactics of harrying the Armada, and using the tides and winds of the Channel to keep the initiative, meant that

107

Overleaf A priest blesses drowning members of the once proud Spanish navy

not one ship under Howard's command was lost. This makes the battle almost unique in English history – especially in view of the size of the engagement. As a contemporary put it, the Spanish "did not, in all their sailing round about England, so much as sink or take one ship, bark, pinnace, or cockboat of ours, or even burn so much as one sheepcote in this land (103)."

A relaxed general

The Duke of Parma's army still threatened from its bases around Dunkirk; the English army waited tensely for any news. But the waiting did not worry one general, Lord Leicester, who was in command of the camp at Colchester. He was enjoying himself, as always: "I am here cook, cater and hunt; for as I myself have not only set the men a-work here about the forts, and was present among them all the first day, but also did peruse and choose the ground fittest for the encamping of the soldiers (104)."

Armada flees north

In the North Sea, the Spanish were in dire straits: "Seeing now that they had lost four or five thousand of their people and having divers maimed and sick persons, and likewise having lost 10 or 12 of their principal ships, they consulted themselves, what they were best to do, being now escaped out of the hands of the English. Their victuals had failed them in like sort, and they began also to want cables, cordage, anchors, masts, sails, and other naval furniture, and utterly despaired of the Duke of Parma's assistance. He was verily hoping and un-doubtedly expecting the return of the Spanish fleet, and was continually occupied about his great preparation, commanding abundance of anchors to be made, and other necessary furniture for a navy to be provided." At last Medina Sidonia decided, "so soon as the wind should serve them, to fetch a compass about Scotland and Ireland, and so to return for Spain (105)."

To return to Spain proved no easy matter. The Armada was in a severely battered state, and short of essential supplies. But neither Norway nor Scotland seemed very promising havens:

"For they well understood, that orders were given throughout all Scotland, that they should not have any succour or assistance there. Neither yet could they in Norway supply their wants. And so having taken certain Scottish and other fisherboats, they brought the men on board their own ships, to be their guides and pilots. Fearing also lest their fresh water should fail them, they cast all their horses and mules overboard. And so, touching nowhere upon the coast of Scotland, but being carried with a fresh gale . . . they proceeded far North, even to 61 degrees of latitude, being at least 40 leagues distant from any land (106)."

On the Scottish coast, the Presbyterians were fearful that the Catholic Spaniards might try to land, and even to seize power in Scotland. One Presbyterian minister, Rev. James Melville, wrote in his memoirs: "Terrible was the fear, piercing were the preachings, earnest, zealous and fervent were the prayers, sounding were the sighs and sobs, and abounding were the tears at that first General Assembly kept at Edinburgh, when the news was credibly told, sometimes of their landing at Dunbar, sometimes at St. Andrews, and in Tay, and now and then at Aberdeen and Cromarty Firth (107)." *Armada threatens Scotland*

Towards the end of 1588, a messenger ran to the Reverend Melville with the news that a Spanish ship had anchored in the harbour, and that its leaders had come ashore. What was to be done? Melville decided to show Christian compassion. The starving Spanish sailors were allowed on shore, and were given kale, porridge and fish to eat, and whatever they could beg from the local householders. *Spaniards given food*

Melville wrote, "Verily all the while my heart melted within for desire of thankfulness to God, when I remembered the proud and cruel nature of their people, and how they would have used us if they had landed with their forces among us . . . We thanked God with our hearts that we had seen them among us in that form (108)."

In a desperate plight, the Duke of Medina Sidonia decided to split the Armada in two. He would try to navigate some of his ships home to Spain, leaving his Vice-Admiral to try and make a landfall with the others in Catholic Ireland. By now the Armada had sailed right around the northern tip of Scotland, and was making its way towards the Atlantic coast of Ireland. *Armada divided*

The Duke "commanded all his followers to shape their course for Biscay. He himself with 20 or 25 of his ships which were best provided of fresh water and other necessaries, held his course over the open sea and returned safely home. The

111

residue of his ships being about 40 in number, and committed to his Vice-Admiral, fell nearer to the coast of Ireland, intending to sail for Cape Clare, because they hoped there to get fresh water, and to refresh themselves on land.

"But after they were driven with many contrary winds, at length, upon the 2nd September, they were cast by a tempest arising from the southwest upon divers parts of Ireland, where many of their ships perished. And among others, the ship of Michael de Oquendo, which was one of the great galleasses, and two great ships of Venice the *La Ratta* and *Belanzara*, with other 36 or 38 ships more, perished in sundry tempests, together with most of the persons contained in them (109)."

Great Spanish losses

The Armada had been the greatest war fleet ever to threaten England. Now it was utterly broken and smashed. The losses were summarised by Richard Hakluyt: "Of the 91 great galleons and hulks there were missing 58, and 33 returned: of the *pataches* and *zabraes* 17 were missing, and 18 returned home. In brief, there were missing 81 ships, in which number were galleasses, galleys, galleons, and other vessels both great and small. And among the 53 ships remaining, those also are reckoned which returned home before they came into the English Channel. Two galleons of those which returned, were by misfortune burnt as they rode in the haven; and such mishaps did many others undergo. Of 30,000 persons which went in this expedition, there perished – according to the number and proportion of the ships – the greater and better part. And many of them which came home, by reason of the toils and inconveniences which they sustained in this voyage, died not long after their arrival (110)."

The ruined Duke

No one could have envied the proud aristocrat, the Duke of Medina Sidonia, his reception when he finally returned home to Spain, and to the wrath of his royal master. He was "deposed from his authority, commanded to his private house, and forbidden to repair to the Court. He could hardly satisfy or yield a reason to his malicious enemies and backbiters (111)."

Opposite Philip II receives the terrible news of the Armada's defeat

Sir John Hawkins, one of the English naval commanders knighted for
his part in the battle

11 Prayers and Rejoicings

IN ENGLAND, the nation turned to prayer. The most heartfelt *Puritan relief* prayers were those of the Puritans, who had had most to fear from a conquest of England by the greatest Catholic power in the world: "While this wonderful and powerful navy was sailing along the English coasts, and all men did now plainly see and hear that which before they would not be persuaded of, all people throughout England prostrated themselves with humble prayers and supplications unto God.

"So especially did the outlandish Churches, who had greatest cause to fear, and against whom by name, the Spaniards had threatened most grievous torments. They called their people to continual fastings and supplications, that they might turn away God's wrath and fury now imminent upon them for their sins, knowing right well that prayer was the only refuge against all enemies and calamities (112)."

It was difficult to know what to do with the Spaniards who *Care of* had been taken prisoner. The greatest nobles could be ransomed *prisoners* in time-honoured fashion: that presented no problem. But what to do with the ordinary sailors and soldiers? – they were worth very little in ransom, even if relatives could be found in Spain to pay for them. Nearly 400 men were captured on the *Nuestra Senora del Rosario*. These were sent to Devon, being the nearest county to their place of capture. The prisoners were put in charge of two local justices of the peace, who complained bitterly to the Privy Council:

"We would have been very glad they had been made water spaniels [drowned] when they were first taken. Their provision, which is left to sustain them, is very little and nought, their fish savours [stinks] . . . and their bread full of worms. The people's charity unto them, coming with so wicked an intent, is very cold; so that if there be not order forthwith taken by your Lordship, they must starve (113)."

Cost of prisoners

Keeping the prisoners cost money, and the Devon justices sent on accounts to the Council. These were some of the items for which they wanted compensation (114):

"For guarding and watching of the Spaniards two nights and a day at their landing = £1 10s.

"For wood to dress the Spanish prisoners' meat ashore = £1

"For eight boats for carrying victuals sundry times to the Spanish prisoners = £2."

At length, the English government agreed that all these prisoners should be ransomed for a month's pay each, to be paid by the Duke of Parma, and Valdez.

Salvage for repairs

After the great events of 1588, the Navy found itself acutely short of the most basic supplies – cables, ropes, anchors, spikes, nails and masts. One Spanish ship, the *San Salvador*, had sunk near Weymouth, and an Admiralty official at Portsmouth called John Thomas wrote to Lord Howard at the Admiralty that he was trying to salvage what he could for the Navy:

"I have been westward, to belay all such masts, yards, shrouds and small ropes or sails that should come ashore, to be kept for the Queen's use or any of her two pinnaces. Their anchors, and please your Honour, there are marks taken where they lie, and I have given order that if they may have any fair weather they will sweep for them. There are four which weigh 3,000 apiece, which I hope will help to requite this charge (115)."

Seamen paid off

In the autumn of 1588, the time came to discharge the men who had served in Lord Howard's fleet. It had cost Queen Elizabeth a huge fortune every day to keep the fleet at sea. Now came the reckoning. It was the job of Sir John Hawkins to issue the Navy pay. Lord Burghley seems to have reproached Hawkins about his handling of this matter, for Hawkins wrote to him:

"I am sorry I do live so long to receive so sharp a letter from your Lordship, considering how carefully I take care to do all for the best and ease charges." He had paid and discharged all the

A medal struck to commemorate the English victory over the Spanish Armada

ships under his immediate responsibility. "I could hardly row from ship to ship, the weather hath been continually so frightful." Four clerks helped him, and Sir William Winter and Edward Fenton.

"Some are discharged with fair words. Some are so miserable and needy, that they are helped with tickets to the victuallers for some victual to help them home; and some with a portion of money, such as my Lord Admiral will appoint, to relieve their sick men and to relieve some of the needy sort, and to avoid an outcry . . .

"The check book of every ship is kept not by me, I assure your Lordship; it is impossible for me to spare time to peruse them. But when the officers put their hands to confirm the pay books, I give my men allowance of so much money as the book maintains; and with that her Majesty is charged and no more . . . If I had any enemy, I would wish him no more harm than the course of my troublesome and painful life (116)."

At the end of November, 1588, the people of England gave themselves over to a national thanksgiving for their deliverance. *Thanksgiving* Hakluyt tells us of "a solemn festival day publicly appointed, wherein all persons were called to resort to the Church, and there to render thanks and praises unto God . . . This solemnity

117

Queen Elizabeth going to St. Paul's Cathedral for a service of thanks-giving after the defeat of the Spanish

was observed upon the 29th November, which day was wholly spent in fasting, prayer, and giving of thanks.

"Likewise the Queen's Majesty herself, imitating the ancient Romans, rode into London in triumph, in thanks for her own and her subjects' glorious deliverance. Attended upon very solemnly by all the principal estates and officers of her realm, she was carried through her City of London in a triumphant chariot, and in robes of triumph, from her Palace to the Cathedral Church of Saint Paul, out of the which the ensigns and colours of the vanquished Spaniards hung displayed.

"And all the Citizens of London in their Liveries stood on either side the street, by their several companies, with their ensigns and banners: and the streets were hung on both sides with blue cloth, which, together with the banners, gave a very stately and gallant prospect. Her Majesty being entered into the Church, together with her clergy and nobles, gave thanks to God, and caused a public sermon to be preached before her at Paul's Cross . . . And with her own princely voice she most Christianly exhorted the people to do the same: at which the people with a loud acclamation wished her a most long and happy life, to the confusion of her foes.

"Thus the magnificent, huge, and mighty fleet of the Spaniards . . . in the year 1588 vanished into smoke (117)."

The greatest threat to the security of England for 500 years had been triumphantly averted.

Glossary

CARAVEL Small light fast ship, often used for sighting or carrying messages

CULVERIN Can mean either a large cannon, or a small firearm

DUCAT A gold coin, worth roughly £1 or $2.50 in modern currency

FIREWORK Explosive shot

GALLEASS Galleon, large sailing ship

GALLEY Single deck ship with sails and oarsmen

HALBERT Weapon with a combined spear-head and axe

ORDNANCE Guns, artillery

PARTISAN Light irregular soldier

PINNACE Small boat with eight oarsmen, usually attached to a large war ship

QUINTAL Unit of weight, about a hundredweight

REAL A small silver coin worth about five pence, or ten cents

ROAD Stretch of coastal water where ships can lie at anchor

ROUNDEL Circular formation

SHALOP Light open boat

SHOAL Submerged sandbanks or rocks which show at low tide

ZABRAE Regiment of soldiers

List of Sources

(1) Quoted J. Hadfield, *Time to Finish the Game*
(2) Richard Hakluyt, *Voyages* (Everyman Edition)
(3) Letter of Don Francisco de Zarate to Don Martino Enriquez
(4) Letter of Sir Francis Drake to Walsingham, 27th April, 1587, quoted in *Navy Records Society.* XI, 107
(5) Quoted Hadfield, 69
(6) Quoted Hirschfield, *The Spanish Armada* (Macdonald), 42
(7) *Ibid*, 100
(8) Quoted Thomas Wright, *Queen Elizabeth and Her Times* (1828), Vol. 2
(9) Quoted J. J. Keevil, *Medicine and the Navy*
(10) *Ibid*
(11) *Ibid*
(12) *Ibid*
(13) *The Art of Shooting ... in Artillery*, Cyprian Lucar (contemp.)
(14) *Ibid*
(15) Richard Hawkyns,
Observations (n.d.)
(16) *Monson's Tracts*, 239
(17) *Ibid*
(18) *Ibid*
(19) Thomas Platter, *Travels in England* (1599)
(20) Sir Walter Raleigh, *History of the World*, Pt. I, Bk. V., Chap. 1
(21) *Monson's Tracts*, 268
(22) *Ibid*
(23) *Ibid*
(24) Quoted Hadfield, *op. cit.*
(25) Quoted Hadfield, *op. cit.*
(26) Quoted Hadfield, 83
(27) *Navy Records Society.* I, 79
(28) *Ibid*, I, 83
(29) *Ibid.* I, 81
(30) *Ibid.* I, 123
(31) *Ibid*
(32) *Ibid*
(33) *Ibid*
(34) Quoted Hadfield, 89
(35) Hakluyt, *Voyages*
(36) *Ibid*
(37) *Ibid*
(38) Richard Hawkyns, *Observations* (n.d., contemp.)
(39) Hakluyt, *Voyages*
(40) Instructions to the
Duke of Medina Sidonia, 1st April, 1588 (*Spanish State Papers*)
(41) Hakluyt, *Voyages*
(42) *Ibid*
(43) *Ibid*
(44) Giovanno Mocenigo, Venetian Ambassador to France, to the Doge and Senate of Venice, 8th April, 1588 (*Venetian State Papers*)
(45) Giovanni Gritti, Venetian Ambassador in Rome, to the Doge and Senate of Venice, 20th August, 1588 *(Venetian State Papers*)
(46) Hakluyt, *Voyages*
(47) *Ibid*
(48) *Ibid*
(49) *Ibid*
(50) Quoted Hirschfield, *op. cit.*
(51) Hakluyt, *Voyages*
(52) *Ibid*
(53) Quoted Hirschfield, *op. cit.*, 73
(54) Medina Sidonia to Juan de Idiaquez, 16th February, 1588 (*Spanish State Papers*)

(55) Quoted Hadfield, 85
(56) Quoted Hirschfield, 73
(57) Quoted Hadfield, 85
(58) *Ibid*, 87
(59) Hakluyt, *Voyages*
(60) Quoted Hadfield, 60
(61) *Ibid*
(62) Hakluyt, *Voyages*
(63) Quoted Hadfield, 94
(64) *Ibid*
(65) *Navy Records Society*, I, 217
(66) *Ibid*
(67) Hakluyt, *Voyages*
(68) *Ibid*
(69) *Ibid*
(70) *Ibid*
(71) *Ibid*
(72) *Ibid*
(73) *Ibid*
(74) *Ibid*
(75) *Ibid*

(76) *Ibid*
(77) *Ibid*
(78) Quoted Hadfield, 122
(79) Hakluyt, *Voyages*
(80) *Ibid*
(81) *Ibid*
(82) *Ibid*
(83) *Ibid*
(84) *Ibid*
(85) *Navy Records Society*, I, 340
(86) *Ibid*, I, 341
(87) Hakluyt, *Voyages*
(88) *Ibid*
(89) *Navy Records Society*, I, 354
(90) Raleigh, *History of the World*, Pt. I, Bk. V
(91) *Ibid*
(92) Quoted Hadfield, 164
(93) *Ibid*, 165
(94) Hakluyt, *Voyages*
(95) *Ibid*

(96) *Ibid*
(97) *Ibid*
(98) *Ibid*
(99) *Ibid*
(100) *Ibid*
(101) Quoted Hadfield, 158
(102) *Navy Records Society*, II, 96
(103) Quoted Hadfield
(104) *Ibid*, 156
(105) Hakluyt, *Voyages*
(106) *Ibid*
(107) Quoted Hadfield, 194
(108) *Ibid*, 195
(109) Hakluyt, *Voyages*
(110) *Ibid*
(111) *Ibid*
(112) *Ibid*
(113) Quoted Hadfield, 207
(114) *Ibid*, 208
(115) *Ibid*, 206
(116) *Ibid*, 206
(117) Hakluyt, *Voyages*

Table of Dates

1534   Act of Supremacy. The English Church has the King as its head instead of the Pope

1554   Philip of Spain marries Mary Tudor (Queen Mary I of England)

1556   Philip accedes to the Spanish throne as Philip II

1558   Queen Elizabeth comes to the English throne on the death of Mary Tudor

1568   Mary, Queen of Scots and Catholic leader, is imprisoned by Elizabeth I

1570   Pope Pius V excommunicates Elizabeth I

1571   Battle of Lepanto: Spain wins a great naval victory over the Turks

1572   France joins Spain in a Catholic alliance against the Protestant nations

1579   Philip II of Spain supports an Irish Catholic rebellion against England

1580   Sir Francis Drake returns from his famous voyage around the world in the *Golden Hind*

1586   Sir Francis Drake captures Santa Domingo from Spain. Philip II begins to build the Armada for war with England. Elizabeth I executes Mary Queen of Scots as result of a Catholic conspiracy

1587   Drake makes his famous raid on the Spanish base at Cadiz – "singeing the King of Spain's beard"

1588   Death of Marquis de Santa Cruz, who is replaced as commander of the Armada by the Duke of Medina Sidonia. The Armada sets out in May, and is finally smashed in July and August

1598   Death of Philip II

1603   Death of Elizabeth I

Picture Credits

The authors and publishers wish to thank all those who have kindly given permission for the reproduction of the illustrations on the following pages: Trustees of the British Museum, 24, 25, 26, 27, 28; British Travel Association, *frontispiece*, 72; J. R. Freeman, 29; the London Museum, 23; Mansell collection, 10, 13, 15, 17, 20, 32, 36–37, 52–53, 60, 61, 63, 76–77, 82–83, 86–87, 88, 90–91, 94–95, 101, 103, 110, 112, 115, 116; Radio Times Hulton Picture Library, 16, 39, 42, 48–49, 58, 62, 68–69, 98, 106–107. All other pictures are in the possession of the Wayland Picture Library.

Further Reading

K. R. Andrews, *Drake's Voyages* (London, Weidenfeld, 1967; New York, Charles Scribner, 1968)

S. T. Bindoff, *Tudor England* (London, Pelican, 1950; Baltimore, Penguin, 1950)

Michael Lewis, *The Spanish Armada* (London, Batsford, 1960; New York, Thomas Crowell, 1968)

Robert Marx, *The Battle of the Spanish Armada* (London, Rupert Hart-Davis, 1968; New York, World Publishing, 1965)

John Masefield (Introduction), *Hakluyt's Voyages* (London, Dent, 1927; New York, Dutton, 1927)

Grant Uden, *Drake at Cadiz* (London, Macdonald, 1969)

Index

128